The Authorities

Powerful Wisdom from Leaders in the Field

JASON G. CHAN

Award Winning Author

ISBN - 978-1-77277-237-1

Publisher
Authorities Press
Markham, ON
Canada

Printed in the United States and Canada.

FOREWORD

Experts are to be admired for their knowledge, but they often remain unrecognized by the general public because they save their information and insights for paying customers and clients. There are many experts in a given field, but their impact is limited to the handful of people with whom they work.

Unlike experts, authorities share their knowledge and expertise far more broadly, so they make a big impact on the world. Authorities become known and admired as leading experts and, as such, typically do very well economically and professionally. Most authorities are also mature enough to know that part of the joy of monetary success is the accompanying moral and spiritual obligation to give back.

Many people want to learn and work with well-respected and generous authorities, but don't always know where to find them. They may be known to their peers, or within a specific community, but have not had the opportunity to reach a wider audience. At one time, they might have submitted a proposal to the For Dummies or Chicken Soup for the Soul series of books, but it's now almost impossible to get accepted as a new author in such branded book series.

It is more than fitting that Raymond Aaron, an internationally known and respected authority in his own right, would be the one to recognize the need for a new venue in which authorities could share their considerable knowledge with readers everywhere. As the only author ever to be included in both of the book series mentioned above, Raymond has had the opportunity to give back and he understands how crucial it is for authorities to have a platform from which to share their expertise.

I have known and worked with Raymond for a number of years and consider him a valued friend and talented coach. He knows how to spot talented and knowledgeable people and he desires to see them prosper. Over the years, success coaching and speaking engagements around the world have made it possible for Raymond to meet many of these talented authorities. He recognizes and relates to their passion and enthusiasm for what they do, as well as their desire to share what they know. He tells me that's why he created this new nonfiction branded book series, The Authorities.

Dr. Nido Qubein
President, High Point University

TABLE OF CONTENTS

Introduction V

Investment Success and Successful Beliefs 1
Jason G. Chan

Step Into Greatness 21
Les Brown

Branding Small Business 31
Raymond Aaron

Sex, Love and Relationships 45
Dr. John Gray

Unstoppable 51
Derek G. Chan

Project Management 69
Gustavo A. Valenzuela

Above and Beyond 97
Dr. Marylyn Poynter

Romancing Your Way Through Network Marketing 105
Dorcas Tay

Buy Your Neighbour's House 115
Brian Klodt

Twice The Retirement For Half The Effort 133
Dr. James McQuiston

Honor Your Inner Treasures 145
Celina Tio

Awakening Your Healer Within 163
Philip Young

INTRODUCTION

This book introduces you to *The Authorities* — individuals who have distinguished themselves in life and in business. Authorities make a big impact on the world. Authorities are leaders in their chosen fields. Authorities typically do very well financially, and are evolved enough to know that part of the joy of monetary success is the accompanying social, moral and spiritual obligation to give back.

Authorities are not just outstanding. They are also *known* to be outstanding.

This additional element begins to explain the difference between two strategic business and life concepts — one that seems great, but isn't, and the other that fills in the essential missing gap of the first.

The first concept is "the expert."

What is an expert? The real definition is …

EXPERT: *a person who knows stuff*

People who have attained a very senior academic degree (like a PhD or an MD) definitely know stuff. People who read voraciously and retain what they read definitely know stuff. Unfortunately, just because you know stuff does not mean that anyone respects the fact that you do. Even though some experts are successful, alas, most are not — because knowing stuff is not enough.

Well, then, what is the missing piece?

What the expert lacks, "the authority" has. The authority both knows stuff and is *known* to know stuff. So, more simply …

AUTHORITY: *a person who is known as an expert*

The difference is not subtle. The difference is not merely semantic. The difference is enormous.

When it comes to this subject, there are actually three categories in which people fall:

- People who don't know much and are unsuccessful in life and in business. Most people fall in this category.
- People who know stuff, but still don't leave much of a footprint in the world. There are a lot of people like this.
- Experts who are also *known* as experts become authorities and authorities are always wondrously successful. Authorities are able to contribute more to humanity through both their chosen work and their giving back.

This book is about the highest category, *The Authorities* — people who have reached the peak in their field and are known as such.

You will definitely know some of *The Authorities* in this book, especially since there are some world-famous ones. Others are just as exceptional, but you may not yet know about them. Our featured author, Jason G. Chan, is one of these authors. Jason is a Certified Life Coach who specializes in finance and investments. With over 10 years investment experience working in the investment industry at one of Canada's largest financial institutions, he has been recognized as National Top Advisor for multiple years for helping and educating others with their finances and investment portfolios. Born in Scarborough, a suburb of Toronto, Ontario, he attended the York-Sheridan Program in Design at York University and Sheridan College where he studied, psychology, philosophy, information design, visual communication and graphic design. From the Faculty of Fine Arts, Jason earned a Bachelors of Design with Honours from the specialized program which had a curriculum that emphasized innovation, creativity and strategic thinking.

After his education, Jason worked briefly as a graphic designer. Since his family had been financially stressed since his early adolescent life, Jason felt it was important to get started with a healthy habit of saving and investing. Unsure how to invest, Jason began reading financial and investment books. Eventually he went on to studying many investment industry licensing courses for his own knowledge and reference. Before long, Jason decided if he was to learn about finance and investments he would get a better and more well rounded experience if he worked at a financial or investment institution. He believed it would be a great opportunity to learn as well as help others along the way. At 26, Jason began his second career as an investment representative at one of Canada's largest financial institutions. He was studying to be a Financial Planner when his father suddenly passed away—two days before his exam. Jason had to visit and deal with many financial institutions such as banks and investment firms to wrap up his father's estate. Shocked and grossly appalled by the type of sales and investment advice he was receiving from supposed investment professionals and peers, Jason was so turned off by the investment industry that he did not want to be a part of it anymore and nearly quit his job.

Burdened knee-deep with student loans as well as his family being heavily entrenched in debt, quitting was not a viable idea. However, with his confidence in the financial and investment industry disturbingly shaken at 27, Jason decided it was important to take personal responsibility for managing his family's finances and investments. Jason adapted his visual communication and graphic arts skill set to technical analysis and applied effective hedge fund strategies towards his investments in the financial markets. Jason made his first million dollars investing in the stock market when he was just shy of 30 years of age, with his second million following shortly after.

They are *The Authorities*. Learn from them. Connect with them. Let them uplift you. Learning from them and working with them is the secret ingredient for success which may well allow you to rise to the level of Authority soon.

To be considered for inclusion in a subsequent edition of *The Authorities*, register to attend a future event at www.aaron.com/events where you will be interviewed and considered.

Investment Success and Successful Beliefs

JASON G. CHAN

"Why are you chuckling to yourself?" my brother asked as we passed by an upscale restaurant one night. "Did I miss something?"

"No, not really," I replied. "Remember those two Ferraris that were waiting for valet parking back by the restaurant that almost everybody who passed by, including us, were looking at and admiring? I just realized that if I wanted to, I could buy both of those Ferraris with cash, one for you and one for me."

Of course, I never did that. But that moment stuck in my head because it was the first time I realized that, financially, I had done okay for myself. I made my first million dollars investing in the stock market when I was just shy of 30 years old. My second million came shortly after that. That's when I stopped counting. I stopped counting because I finally found some comfort in knowing that my family was doing okay and that I was doing okay.

A few years before that, my father had suddenly passed away. It happened in 2008 in the middle of one of the greatest recessions in history. My family was entrenched in debt and my parents hardly had any retirement savings, let alone other investments. My two younger brothers and I were burdened knee-deep in student loan debt. I was living in my parents' living room because the basement where I had been living got flooded and became too moldy to stay in.

For most of my adolescent and early adult life, our family cash flow was tight, and we couldn't even afford a decent study desk. I haven't done too shabby for a boy whose desk was actually nothing more than a door flipped sideways and propped up by four poles on each corner; definitely not too shabby as an investor for someone whose degree was in fine arts and graphic design. I don't have a degree in business, finance or economics. I don't believe we need fancy degrees or education to do well in finance and investments or in life. For those who likes degrees, later in life I was told that I actually got a PhD earlier in life, since I was Poor, Hungry and Driven. At the end of the day, it's not your degrees or titles that make you, it's really about your vision and your beliefs.

YOUR BELIEFS ARE IMPORTANT

Sometimes people ask me what I did or what I invested in, hoping to get some insight as to how they too can achieve what I have. They're usually asking about specific things I did, specific things I invested in, or tools I used. What they don't understand is that these things are not the important part. Belief is where it all starts. To achieve investment success by having the proper successful beliefs, mental concepts, and proper mindset is the key.

After all, we all act and behave in certain ways because of our beliefs. Some beliefs serve us, some limit or deter us, and some set us astray. They shape what we do and how we do it. Before anything even starts, our beliefs tell us what we can do because they shape what we think is possible and what is not. Therefore, having the proper beliefs, or shaping what you already have, is really important in life, and also in investments. My purpose and goal is to help you adopt proper, empowering beliefs and realign, even discard, the negative ones as they relate to investments. It is only with a proper mindset and a successful beliefs system that you can get ahead in finances and achieve sustainable, consistent and long term investment success.

The first and, perhaps, the most important belief I want to share with you is it's possible for you to achieve financial and investment success. Not only can you achieve it, but you can achieve it on your own by empowering yourself to take control of your finances and investments. If a poor boy who started off living in a basement with a door as a study desk, who studied fine arts and graphic design, and who had large student loans and family debt could do it, so could you.

"It's Possible" is one of my favorite phrases from Les Brown. He goes on to describe that one of the keys to changing our belief system and enabling us to act on our dreams is knowing that something is possible. To know that a goal or that dream or that something we want or achieve has already been done or achieved by someone else, is to know that something is possible and achievable. More importantly, that "It's Possible" for you to achieve it too!

UNDERSTANDING FINANCE AND INVESTMENTS IS A LIFE SKILL

One of the first questions people come across when it comes to their finances and investments is, "Should I manage them myself or should I get someone else in the financial industry, such as an investment firm or bank, to manage them for me?"

Not only am I an individual investor who manages my own finances, I have also worked in the financial services industry, for one of the largest financial institutions in the country, as an investment sales representative for over 10 years. I am also a certified life coach who specializes in finance and investments. Through my various experiences, my short answer is that you should eventually invest in yourself and invest for yourself. Being able to take control and take charge of your finances and investments is a very liberating feeling that everyone should enjoy.

The investment service industry has a purpose and a place in everybody's life, but by no means should it be used or regarded as a long-term solution. It's like riding a bicycle with training wheels. Many people dream of financial freedom, but they are often dependent on an investment company to get them there. How could you be free and dependent at the same time?

Understanding finance and investments is a necessity in life. Just like eating and cooking, it's something we have to do for the rest of our lives. For this reason, I believe it's a life skill we should all acquire and develop. We have to deal with money, so we need to understand finance. Unless we spend every dime we earn or put everything under a mattress, we all have to invest. At the end of the day, nobody cares more about your financial future and well-being more than you.

HAVING SOMEONE ELSE MANAGE YOUR MONEY IS MORE COSTLY THAN YOU THINK

When it comes to eating, we won't eat out every meal, every day for the rest of our lives. We won't do that because we know it doesn't make sense and it gets expensive. So why would it make sense to pay someone else or a company to manage your investments every day for the rest of your life? Well, many people actually do that. One of the main reasons is because the investment industry has presented their fees in a way that seems deceivingly small and inexpensive. That's why many people don't mind "dining out" their whole lives.

Let's use the mutual fund industry as an example. The mutual fund industry is what most people are exposed to and familiar with when it comes to professional investment management. Aside from possible front-load and back-load fees and commissions, all mutual funds charge what they call a management expense ratio or MER. The MER alone for the average mutual fund ranges from approximately 2% - 2.5% a year. We'll take the low end of 2% to give them the benefit of the doubt. A 2% annual fee sounds small and nominal, doesn't it? The financial industry usually does not take the time or effort to explain what this fee actually means. Often customers are left with the impression that they get charged 2% MER from the gains that the company makes for them, if any.

In reality, that 2% MER is calculated and charged based on the entire amount of money they are managing for the customer, or what they call assets under management. What that means is, if you give them $100 to invest, they will charge you 2% on that $100, so essentially $2. Say you have $100,000 invested with them. At 2% MER, that works out to be $2,000 a year. For those who wish to have $1,000,000 ($1 Million dollars) a 2% MER would cost them $20,000 a year! To look at it from another perspective, a 2% MER fee in 5 years alone, works out to 10% (2% x 5). In 10 years, that works out to be 20% (2% x 10). In a mere 5 years and 10 years respectively, you would have paid out 10% and 20% of your hard-earned money in MER fees. Now consider that most people save and invest for retirement for about 35 years, how does the math work out for a long duration like that?

As I mentioned, the financial and investment industry is a business. Just like the restaurant industry and eating out, there is a time and place for services like that. However, it should not be used as a long-term solution, because it becomes very costly in the long run. I feel a true investment company and professional should be promoting financial freedom and independence, not financial dependence. Understanding finance and investments is truly a life skill that we should all acquire and develop. We can't afford not to.

In the examples above, I purposely kept the math simple and to the point and avoided financial jargon, such as compounding, time value, etc., because those are the kind of things that deter from the basic idea and confuse clients. The investment industry will critique our example and try to say that they will grow the client's money through the years. However, at the end of day, they cannot guarantee you any gains. So we won't factor that in. And to be fair, I won't assume they'll lose your money either. I kept it neutral in my example—no gains, no losses—similar to the "lost decade" that we experienced in the stock markets not too long ago.

INVESTING IS LIKE TREASURE HUNTING

When most people think of the world of investments and finance it seems overwhelmingly complex. A simple and interesting analogy I use to compare the world of investing and the investment industry is a big treasure hunt. If we were to look at it from this perspective, we would get a better understanding of how things work, many things would become apparent and begin to make sense.

So off to treasure hunting we go. Imagine we are in a world where treasure hunting is a big deal and almost everybody is out to find some treasure. Opinions on how to find treasure are a dime a dozen and everybody has their ideas and opinions.

Yet, despite the abundance of ideas and strategies floating around, many of these ideas tend to be passed around by people who have never found any significant treasure themselves. They hear and get these ideas and concepts from family members, a friend, a friend of a friend, and various media outlets. And where did many of these ideas originate from? A lot of these ideas actually came about through the "treasure hunting industry."

Yes, treasure hunting is such a big deal, there's actually a treasure hunting industry which is supposedly there to help you and guide you to find treasure. There are big corporate institutions with many employees who sell you treasure maps, treasure guides, strategies, tools and gadgets along with various products and services which they claim will help you find treasure. Many of them offer packaged plans to help treasure hunt for you through their professional and experienced treasure hunters.

The deal is that you put up all the capital to be used for the treasure hunt, but they do not guarantee you any success. The only guarantee is that they will charge you a management fee whether or not they find you treasure. And if they do end up finding treasure, they actually take a bigger cut of your money. So you put up all the money and take all the risk and they take a risk free payment from you in order to help you treasure hunt. And there are no guarantees of success. It's a pretty good business model for them, but not such a good business idea for you.

At some point you might begin to wonder that if these companies and their staff are so good at treasure hunting, how come they just don't focus on that and treasure hunt for themselves? Eventually, you'll realize that these companies actually make money from selling treasure hunting packages and products and by providing treasure hunting services. They don't make their money from actually finding treasure, per se.

Their frontline staff, sales representatives and professional treasure hunters, can give you all sorts of treasure hunting advice, ideas, and strategies, along with various treasure products and services the company has to offer. However, like most regular people, most of them have never found success in treasure hunting. The majority of their income actually comes from working their sales jobs and earning commission selling treasure hunting packages, products and services.

Sometimes you see some of these sales people enjoying the luxuries of life which can create the impression that they have actually found treasure from treasure hunting, but the reality is, they were actually just a successful sales person, not a successful treasure hunter.

Remember how we said that much of the common investment advice that floats around in public originated from these treasure hunting companies in the treasure hunting industry? A lot of the time this supposed treasure hunting advice is actually based on half-truths that are either outdated, have lost effectiveness, or have never been useful at all. They are mainly ideas and strategies used to promote and sell various treasure hunting packages, products and services.

There are actually really good and skillful treasure hunters out there. As you would expect, most of them spend their time treasure hunting for themselves. Some do open up treasure hunting companies to help others find treasure, but they usually require clients with lots of money and many of them have reached capacity and have stopped taking on new clients.

Keep this treasure hunting analogy in mind the next time you think about investments and the investment industry. It should give you an idea of how to make sense of it all and help you decide if you really wish to have someone else treasure hunt for you or not.

THE INVESTMENT LANDSCAPE HAS CHANGED

Since the new millennium, the stock market and investment landscape has been a lot different than it was in previous decades. This is not just a belief—it is a fact. It is important that we recognize and acknowledge this reality and incorporate it into our belief system for two main reasons.

First of all, in order to invest successfully and navigate through the stock market, we need to understand what kind of landscape and environment we are currently in. Imagine you are taking a road trip, how could you expect a to get from point A to point B if you were using an old and dated road map from many decades ago? I am sure it would be a frustrating trip with a few wrong turns here and there.

Secondly, understanding how the stock market and investment landscape used to be can help us understand where many investment ideas and strategies we still hear and read about came to be. More important is why they have lost relevance, effectiveness and significance.

Using the beginning of the new millennium, the year 2000, as a benchmark for the midpoint year of reference, let us take a look at the last 36 years of the S&P500, a popular and widely followed North American stock index. We will take a look and compare the 18 years prior to the new millennium and 18 years since the new millennium. So from 1982 to 2000, compared to 2000 to 2018.

In terms of returns, if you were to just buy and hold from the beginning of 1982 to the beginning of 2000, the 18 years prior to 2000, the total return of the S&P 500 was approximately 1,100%. From the beginning of 2000 to the beginning of 2018, the last 18 years, the total return of the S&P 500 was approximately 92%. A 1,110% return compared to a 92% return. That's a difference of almost 12 times.

In terms of declines and recovery, between 1982 and 2000, the two biggest drops were Black Monday of 1987, which saw an approximately 36% drop from top to bottom, which took 8 months to break even, and August of 1998 which saw an approximately 23% drop from top to bottom, which took less than 2 months to break even.

In terms of declines and recovery, between 2000 and 2018, the two biggest drops were an approximately 50% drop during the years from early 2000 to early 2003. If you happened to have bought at the peak, it would have taken you about 7.5 years to break even. Then an approximately 57% drop from mid 2007 to early 2009. If you happened to have bought at the peak, it would have taken you about 6 years to break even.

From 1982 to 2000, there was a 23% to 36% drop, with a recovery time of 2 to 8 months, compared to the years from 2000 to 2018, in which there was a 50% to 57% drop, with a recovery time of 6 to 7.5 years. From declines to recoveries, there was a dramatic difference in magnitude.

To summarize, it is important that we recognize and acknowledge that the investment landscape has changed a lot in the last 20 years because many investment strategies and ideologies we still hear today were developed during that comparatively stable and less volatile time. However, due to the changes we have seen in the last 20 years, many of these strategies and ideologies have lost their effectiveness, value, and relevance. The conclusion is, since our investment landscape has changed and evolved, we too need to evolve and adapt our investment strategies to the present. We cannot just keep on blindly using what has worked in the past.

WE INVEST IN OUR BELIEFS, NOT THE MARKETS

As we started off by mentioning, beliefs are very important when it comes to investing. They affect how we invest: if we take charge of our investments ourselves, have someone else invest for us or if we even invest at all. More importantly, I have to stress the importance of adopting the right and proper beliefs because ultimately when we are investing, we are investing in our beliefs. People often think they are investing in the markets, but actually what they are investing in is their beliefs about the markets. This is a critical concept to keep in mind. Personally, understanding and realizing that concept helped take my investments to the next level.

This reality might be a little difficult to wrap our heads around at first, but consider this, the markets behave the same for everyone. If we are just investing in the markets, we should all get similar if not identical results. But we don't. How come some people make more money than others in a rising market, for example? Or how come some are able to profit from a recession while others lose a fortune? The market's behaviour and performance does not vary from one person to another. It is the beliefs about the markets that vary from one person to another. Therefore, one of the main keys to being able to invest successfully is to have the proper beliefs in regards to investing and the markets.

GENUINE INVESTMENT ADVICE AND POOR INVESTMENT ADVICE

Many of our beliefs regarding investments have been acquired and shaped by various pieces of investment advice we've come across over time. And there's all sorts of investment concepts, strategies, and theories. Which ones serves us? Which ones do not? There was a time when it was tough getting information, let alone getting information in a timely manner. But today, with the evolution of technology via computers, smartphones and the internet, we live in a time of information overload. Investment ideas and strategies are a dime a dozen. Almost everyone seems to have an idea of what to do. We come across so many investment ideas and so much advice. Often, the more we learn the more confused we get, as many of these investment ideas seem to contradict each other. How do we organize and conceptualize them all in a context that makes sense? As an individual investor I, too, had to struggle with that problem.

After years of study, research and practical hands-on experience investing my own money, as well as working in the finance and investment sales industry, I was finally able to sort and put everything in context. This belief system is a mental construct meant to organize all the ideas, advice, theories, strategies, and concepts I've accumulated as they relate to investments. I'll just refer to all of that as "investment advice" for simplicity.

It's obvious there's some investment advice that works and some that does not. So, I separate them into two categories: "Genuine Investment Advice" and "Poor Investment Advice." Within those two categories, there are actually two sub-categories we could further separate the investment advice into.

Within Genuine Investment Advice, the first subcategory is investment advice that I believe is almost universal and works for almost everyone. For example, diversification, cutting losses short, letting winners grow, and waiting for favourable risk to return opportunities before investing.

The second subcategory, as well as all the other categories we'll touch upon, is where things get interesting. It's where it causes lots of confusion among people's belief systems and is a source of frustration for many. Within this second sub-category of Genuine Investment Advice is the investment advice that is accurate and works but may not work for everyone, because it depends on their personality and their investment style. For example, many investment ideas, theories, and strategies seem like complete opposites when you compare them with one another: value investing versus momentum investing, swing trading versus momentum investing, fundamental analysis versus technical analysis, short-term trading versus long-term investing, buy low and sell high versus buy high and sell higher, and top down versus bottom up investment styles. All these investment ideas and strategies work, but success depends on how they match the individual investor's personality and how they are used alongside their investment style. In a nutshell, those are examples of Genuine Investment Advice.

On the other end of the spectrum from Genuine Investment Advice we have Poor Investment Advice. It's basically advice that is not effective or does not work. Within this main category, it also has two sub-categories.

In the first sub-category is investment advice that used to work but is outdated because of the change in the investment landscape that we touched upon earlier. It used to work and perhaps even used to deliver great results but has since greatly lost value and effectiveness. Yet, these investment ideas still get passed around by many people because they have failed to recognize that the investment landscape has dramatically changed and evolved in recent years.

Some examples are: index investing, buying and holding indiscriminately, dollar cost averaging, and investing on a consistent and regular schedule regardless of overall market conditions. It's easy to see where such investment ideas, strategies and advice come from once we understand how the investment landscape used to be and what had happened in the past. Like we've seen in our example, the stock market, namely the S&P500, went up approximately 1,100% from 1982 to the year 2000. Yet, in our recent investment landscape from 2000 to the beginning of 2018, the total return of the S&P500 was a mere 92%—a return that's dramatically less than 1/12th in the same 18-year time span. That is less than 10% of the 1,100% return the we've seen from 1982 to the year 2000.

The second subcategory of Poor Investment Advice is the one which I despise the most. They are essentially "investment advice" that was never effective and never worked. For example, advice such as "If you don't sell your losing position, you aren't really losing money because unless you cash out, it's only a paper loss." That is as foolish as saying "If you go to the casino and convert your cash into casino chips, then you lose your chips, you're not actually losing money unless you convert those chips back into cash." Then there's "Adding to losses and losing positions is beneficial because when you average down, it gives you better value and a lower overall price point." With this strategy, you are not only not cutting your losses, you are adding to an already losing position. Technically, you could use this flawed logic to invest in a company as it goes all the way down to bankruptcy because it suggests the lower the price goes, the more you should invest. There is also "Focus on the long-term, and don't worry that your stocks are down because you're still getting paid dividends." Focusing solely on dividends presents a very distorted and partial picture, as you should be focusing on total return which consists of dividends plus any capital gains or losses. With that in mind, if your stock is down -40%, it would be foolish to say it's alright because you're receiving a 3% dividend yield.

People often ask, "If such investment advice doesn't work, then why do people say these things?" The answer is because these ideas mainly originate and get spread around by unscrupulous individuals in the financial and investment industry. In reality, such investment advice was merely conjured up to promote and sell investment products to customers and keep their customers invested so they could continue to charge them various fees and commissions.

Unfortunately, because much of this investment advice came from individuals within the financial and investment industry, it gave them a false sense of credibility and such bad advice got perpetually circulated. This is especially true because the advice is usually mixed in with some rationalization and half truths. When I say half truths, I am also referring to the dated investment advice that we mentioned earlier. I consider those half truths, because those strategies used to work, but have greatly lost significance since. Nevertheless, such bad advice is still often used as sales pitches by individuals in the industry to promote and sell various investment products.

Notice that all such advice falls under a similar underlying idea. It is to tell the customer that it is always a good time to invest and once they are invested, to never sell. For example, when the markets are high, they will say you should invest more because things are going well and you are making money. When the markets are low, they will say you should invest more because you are getting good value. Also, it is always a good time to invest, regardless of how the overall market condition is, because it is supposedly about your time in the markets, not timing the markets. Basically, the message is always geared at giving them your money, keeping it with them and never taking it away, so they can continuously charge you various fees. At the end of the day, if the client makes money, all the better, but even if they don't, the individual and company still gets to charge their fees.

In providing Genuine Investment Advice verses Poor Investment Advice, an individual's salary and bonus often comes in between the two. I'm reminded of a quote from Upton Sinclair: "It is difficult to get a man to understand something, when his salary depends on his not understanding it." However, to be fair, many of those who work in the financial and investment industry are not unscrupulous or ill-intentioned. Like many everyday people, they too, are caught up in the confusion. They come across poor investment advice that they actually believe to be true, which they use themselves and also end up passing on.

ADDITIONAL INVESTMENT TIPS FOR THE EVERYDAY INVESTOR

Make Use of Technical Analysis

As individual investors, we have limited time and resources. I believe the most efficient and effective way for an individual investor to conduct market research and to look for investment opportunities is through the use of technical analysis. Before you get intimidated, technical analysis is basically a fancy way of saying to look at price charts and graphs. You are literally looking at a picture, the big picture. It's efficient because, for example, if I wanted to, I could literally look through hundreds of companies and their price charts in a day. Comparatively, I cannot read through hundreds of annual reports or articles a day.

Keep an Investing Journal

Experiencing losses due to bad judgements or mistakes is part of every investor's journey. Unfortunately, when it comes to investing, making mistakes usually translates to losing money. At least when losses and mistakes occur, try to profit from them by keeping a journal of what happened and how, in an effort to learn from the experience and to not to let it happen again. As the saying goes, "Fool me once, shame on you. Fool me twice, shame on me."

Be Sure to Diversify

Diversification is a simple risk management technique we should all make use of to protect ourselves from the unknown and to improve our risk to return ratio. The simple reason being we can never foresee and predict everything in the markets. During my years of investing, I've seen an oil company whose oil rig was destroyed by a natural disaster; a factory that, due to some employee's negligence, was burned down to a crisp; the CEO of a company who got caught up in various alleged scandals leading to the collapse of the company and, one of my favorites, which is when Tesla's stock price took a sudden dive one day because Elon Musk decided to announce that the company was going bankrupt as an April Fool's Day joke in 2018. No matter how much in-depth research we conduct, nobody could have foreseen any of those events happening. So protect your investment portfolio by diversifying.

Look Beyond "Glam Stocks"

When individuals share their investment holdings with me, I often notice that they have many of the same stock holdings. The reason is they often have what I call "Glam Stocks." These are the glamorous stocks we often hear about in the news and media, the ones our friends and family talk about at dinner parties and gatherings. There is nothing wrong with having those holdings per se, but expand your scope, look further and dig deeper. You will realize that there are plenty of more diverse opportunities out there, many of which are either less volatile and less risky, have more growth potential, have a better performance record or sometimes all of the above. So keep looking and don't settle just for what you hear or see around you.

Know When to Get Out, Before You Get In

Before you get into an investment position, decide when you would exit if things do not go as intended. You are more clear minded before you start an investment. So decide when you would exit if things do not go your way ahead of time, as you will lose objectivity afterwards.

Gradually Ease In and Out of Investments

When investing, especially in stocks, a common practice is to use one entry and one exit into an investment position. Instead of using an all-in or all-out approach, a more strategic risk management approach would be to gradually ease yourself in and out of an investment depending on its subsequent performance. For example, instead of investing $5,000 all at once, consider investing initially only $2,500, then decide if you still want to invest the remaining $2,500 depending on the subsequent performance of the particular investment. Doing this would automatically cut your initial risk by 50%. The same idea applies to getting out of an investment.

Cut Losses and Keep Them Small

When investing, keeping control of our losses is a vital component of risk management. If there is one common piece of advice I've gathered from many great investors, it is that they all cut their losses and keep them small. Considering that most big losses usually started off as small losses, there is no point in letting a small loss grow into a big loss. If you are uncertain about an investment holding, instead of holding all of it or none of it, consider selling a portion of it. For example, if you sell half of it, you will reduce your risk by 50%. Another common culprit that leads investors to hold onto losses is focusing on break-even points and prices. In reality, nobody actually cares where or at what price you bought an investment and where you would break-even. It has no special meaning to anybody other than you and the tax department, so do not focus on that.

Avoid Adding to Losing Positions

When you have a losing investment position, often people believe that buying more will get you better value as you average down your overall price point. That is actually a poor strategy because having a losing position usually means that something you anticipated did not materialize and instead the opposite outcome occurred. There must have been something that was misjudged, overlooked, or unforeseen. Therefore, it does not make strategic sense to add more to an investment which you have already misunderstood and misjudged. Moreover, not only does that go against the concept of keeping your losses small, it is in fact the opposite, because you are adding more money to a losing position.

Remember that You Are Investing in Your Beliefs, Not the Markets

If there is one piece of advice that is more important than controlling your losses, it would definitely be that nobody cares more about your financial well-being than you. So understanding finance and investments is a life skill you should not only acquire but develop, and it all starts with your beliefs. At the core of it all, it is about working on developing your investment belief system.

This requires realigning and readjusting your beliefs and perhaps adopting new ones that serve you, while discarding those that do not. Remember that at the end of the day, we are all just investing in our beliefs.

FINAL THOUGHTS

Finance and investments are one of my greatest passions. I hope I was able to share some fresh perspectives and unique insights on subjects that I personally find to be rarely touched upon or discussed. The ideas and concepts are not exhaustive or complete, however, these are the big ideas, essential concepts and quintessential core beliefs that I've acquired through the years and which really helped propel my investment understanding and financial success.

Often there is nothing worse than to listen to someone advising you on how to reach your goals, when they have not actually reached it themselves. If there was a way for me to turn back time and have the opportunity to sit down with some successful investors who were willing to give me a few important pointers about finance and investing over a cup of coffee or a meal, I hope they would have shared with me the same pointers and beliefs I have shared with you in the last few pages. I know the insights would have definitely made my investment and financial experience a lot smoother and would have helped me reach my financial goals a lot sooner. These beliefs I'm talking about have helped me through many hurdles, make many investment breakthroughs and achieve financial success. I hope they will do the same for you. Remember, "It's Possible!"

For more investment insight, techniques and strategies, visit:

InvestingItWisely.com

Step Into Greatness

LES BROWN

You have greatness within you. You can do more than you could ever imagine. The problem most people have is that they set a goal and then ask "how can I do it? I don't have the necessary skills or education or experience".

I know what that's like. I wasted 14 years on asking myself how I could be a motivational speaker. My mind focused on the negative—on the things that were in my way, rather than on the things that were not.

It's not what you don't have but what you think you need that keeps you from getting what you want from life. But, when the dream is big enough, the obstacles don't matter. You'll get there if you stay the course. Nothing can stop you but death itself.

Think about that last statement for a minute. There's nothing on this earth that can stop you from achieving what it is that you want. So, get out of your way, and quit sabotaging your dreams. Do everything in your power to make them happen—because you cannot fail!

They say the best way to die is with your loved ones gathered around your bed. But what if you were dying and it was the ideas you never acted upon, the gifts you never used and the dreams you never pursued, that were circled around your bed? Answer that question right now. Write down your answers. If you die this very moment what ideas, what gifts, what dreams will die with you?

Then say: I refuse to die an unlived life! You beat out 40 million sperm to get here, and you'll never have to face such odds again. Walk through the field of life and leave a trail behind.

One day, one of my rich friends brought my mother a new pair of shoes for me. Now, even though we weren't well off, I didn't want them; they were a size nine and I was a size nine and a half. My mother didn't listen and told my sister to go get some Vaseline, which she rubbed all over my feet. Then my mother had me put those shoes on, minding that I didn't scrunch down the heel. She had my sister run some water in the bathtub, and I was told to get in and walk around in the water. I said that my feet hurt. She just ignored me and asked about my day at school, how everything went and did I get into any fights? I knew what she was up to, that she was trying to distract me, so I said I had only gotten into three fights. After a while mother asked me if my feet still hurt. I admitted that the pain had indeed lessened. She kept me walking in that tub until I had a brand new pair of comfortable, size nine and a half shoes.

You see, once the leather in the shoes got wet, they stretched! And what you need to do is stretch a little. I believe that most people don't set high goals and miss them, but rather, they set lower goals and hit them and then they stay there, stuck on the side of the highway of life. When you're pursuing your greatness, you don't know what your limitations are, and you need to act like you don't have any. If you shoot for the moon and miss, you'll still be in the stars.

You also need coaching (a mentor). Why? There are times you, too, will find yourself parked on the side of the highway of life with no gas in the vehicle. What you need then is someone to stop and offer to pick up some gas down the road a ways and bring it back to you. That person is your coach. Yes, they are there for advice, but their main job is to help you through the difficulties that life throws at all of us.

Another reason for having a coach is that you can't see the picture when you're in the frame. In other words, he or she can often see where you are with a clarity and focus that's unavailable to you. They're not going to leave you parked along the road of life, nor are they going to allow you to be stuck in the moment like a photo in a frame.

And let's say you just can't see you're way forward. You don't believe it's possible. Sometimes you just have to believe in someone's belief in you. This could be your coach, a loved one or even a staunch friend. You need to hear them say you can do it, time and again. Because, after all, faith comes from hearing and hearing and hearing.

Look at it this way. Most people fail because of possibility blindness. They can't see what lies before them. There are always possibilities. Because of this, your dream is possible. You may fail often. In fact, I want you to say this: I will fail my way to success. Here is why.

I had a TV show that failed. I felt I had to go back to public speaking. I had failed, so I parked my car for ten years. Then I saw Dr. Wayne Dyer was still on PBS and I decided to call them. They said they would love to work with me and asked where I had been. I wasn't as good as I had been ten years before, as I was out of practice, but I still had to get back in the game. I was determined to drive on empty.

Listen to recordings, go to seminars, challenge yourself, and you'll begin to step into your greatness, you'll begin to fill yourself with the energy you need to climb to ever greater heights. Most people never attend a seminar. They won't invest money in books or audio programs. You put yourself in the top 5 percent just by making a different choice than the average person. This is called contrary thinking. It's a concept taken from the financial industry. One considers choosing the exact opposite behaviour of the average person as a way to get better than average results. You don't have to make the contrarian choice, but if you don't have anything to lose by going that road, why not consider the option?

Make your move before you're ready. Walk by faith not by sight and make sure you're happy doing it. If you can't be happy, what else is there? Helen Keller said, "Life is short, eat the dessert first."

What is faith? Many of us think of God when we think of faith. A different viewpoint claims that faith is a firm belief in something for which there is no proof. I would rather think of faith as something that is believed especially with strong conviction. It is this last definition I am referring to when I say walk by faith not by sight. Be happy and go forth with strong conviction that you are destined for greatness.

An important step on your way to greatness is to take the time to detoxify. You've got to look at the people in your life. What are they doing for you? Are they setting a pace that you can follow? If not, whose pace have you adjusted to? If you're the smartest in your group, find a new group.

Are the people in your life pulling you down or lifting you up? You know what to do, right? Banish the negative and stay with the positive; it's that simple. Dr. Norman Vincent Peale once said (when I was in the audience), "You are special. You have greatness within you, and you can do more than you could ever possibly imagine."

He overrode the inner conversations in my mind and reached the heart of me. He set me on fire. This is yet another reason for seeking out the help of a coach or mentor or other new people in your life. They can do what Dr. Peale did for me. They can set your passion free.

How important is it to have the right kind of person/people on your side? There was a study done that determined it takes 16 people saying you can do something to overcome one person who says you can't do something. That's right, one negative, unsupportive person can wipe out the work of 16 other supportive people. The message can't be any clearer than that.

Let's face the cold, hard truth: most people stay in park along the highway of life. They never feel the passion, the love for their fellow man, or for the work they do. They are stuck in the proverbial rut. What's the reason? There are many reasons, but only one common factor: fear — fear of change, fear of failure, fear of success, fear they may not be good enough, fear of competition, even fear of rejection.

"Rejection is a myth," says Jack Canfield, co-author of The Chicken Soup for the Soul series. "It's not like you get a slap in the face each time you are rejected." Why not take every "no" you receive as a vitamin, and every time you take one know you are another step closer to success.

You will win if you don't quit. Even a broken clock is right twice a day.

Professional baseball players, on average, get on base just three times out of every ten times they face the opposing pitcher. Even superstars fail half of the time they appear at the plate.

Top commissioned salespeople face similar odds. They make may make one sale from every three people they see, but it will have taken them between 75 and 100 telephone calls to make the 15 appointments they need to close their five sales for the week. And these are statistics for the elite. Most salespeople never reach these kinds of numbers.

People don't spend their lives working for just one company anymore. This means you must build up a set of skills and experiences that are portable. This can be done a number of ways, but my favourite approaches follow.

You must be willing to do the things others won't do in order to have tomorrow the things that others don't have. Provide more service than you get paid for. Set some high standards for yourself.

Begin each day with your most difficult task. The rest of the day will seem more enjoyable and a whole lot easier.

Someone needs help with a problem? Be the solution to that problem.

Also, find those tasks that are being consistently ignored and do them. You'll be surprised by the results. An acquaintance of mine used this approach at a number of entry-level positions and each time he quickly ended up being offered a position in management.

You must increase your energy. Kick it up a notch. We are spirits having a physical existence; let your spirit shine. Quit frittering away your energy. Use it to move you closer to the achievement of your dreams. Refuse to spend it on non-productive activities.

What do people say about you when you leave a room? Are you willing to take responsibility—to walk your talk. There is a terrible epidemic sweeping our nation, and it is the refusal to take responsibility for one's actions. Consider that at some point in any situation there will have been a moment where you could have done something to change the outcome. To that end you are responsible for what happened. It's a hard thing to accept, but it's true.

Life's hard. It was hard when I was told I had cancer. I had sunken into despair, and was hiding away in my study when my son came in. My son asked me if I was going to die. What could I do? I told him I was going to fight, even though I was scared. I also told him that I needed some help. Not because I was weak but because I wanted to stay strong. Keep asking until you get help. Don't stop until you get it.

A setback is the setup for a comeback. A setback is simply a misstep on the long road of success. It means nothing in the larger scheme of things. And, surprisingly, it sets you up for your next win. It tends to focus you and your energy on your immediate goals, paving the way for your next sprint, for your comeback.

It's worth it. Your dreams are worth the sacrifices you'll have to make to achieve them. Find five reasons that will make your dreams worth it for you. Say to yourself, I refuse to live an unlived life.

If you are casual about your dreams, you'll end up a casualty. You must be passionate about your dreams, living and breathing them throughout your days. You've got to be hungry! People who are hungry refuse to take no for an answer. Make NO your vitamin. Be unstoppable. Be hungry.

Let me give you an example of what I mean by hungry …

I decided I wanted to become a disc jockey, so I went down to the local radio station and asked the manager, Mr. Milton "Butterball" Smith, if he had a job available for a disc jockey. He said he did not. The next day I went back, and Mr. Smith asked "Weren't you here yesterday?" I explained that I was just checking to see if anyone was sick or had died. He responded by telling me not to come back again. Day three, I went back again—with the same story. Mr. Smith told me to get out of there. I came back the fourth day and gave Mr. Smith my story one more time. He was so beside himself that he told me to get him a cup of coffee. I said, "Yes, sir!" That's how I became the errand boy.

While working as an errand boy at the station, I took every opportunity to hang out with the deejays and to observe them working. After I had taught myself how to run the control room, it was just a matter of biding my time.

Then one day an opportunity presented itself. One of the disc jockeys by the name of Rockin' Roger was drinking heavily while he was on the air. It was a Saturday afternoon. And there I was, the only one there.

I watched him through the control-room window. I walked back and forth in front of that window like a cat watching a mouse, saying "Drink, Rock, Drink!" I was young. I was ready. And I was hungry.

Pretty soon, the phone rang. It was the station manager. He said, "Les, this is Mr. Klein."

I said, "Yes, I know."

He said, "Rock can't finish his program."

I said, "Yes sir, I know."

He said, "Would you call one of the other disc jockeys to fill in?"

I said, "Yes sir, I sure will, sir."

And when he hung up, I said, "Now he must think I'm crazy." I called up my mama and my girlfriend, Cassandra, and I told them, "Ya'll go out on the front porch and turn up the radio, I'M ABOUT TO COME ON THE AIR!"

I waited 15 or 20 minutes and called the station manager back. I said, "Mr. Klein, I can't find NOBODY!"

He said, "Young boy, do you know how to work the controls?"

I said, "Yes, sir."

He said, "Go in there, but don't say anything. Hear me?"

I said, "Yes, sir."

I couldn't wait to get old Rock out of the way. I went in there, took my seat behind that turntable, flipped on the microphone and let 'er rip.

"Look out, this is me, LB., triple P. Les Brown your platter-playin' papa. There were none before me and there will be none after me, therefore that makes me the one and only. Young and single and love to mingle, certified, bona fide and indubitably qualified to bring you satisfaction and a whole lot of action. Look out baby, I'm your LOVE man."

I WAS HUNGRY!

During my adult life I've been a deejay, a radio station manager, a Democrat in the Ohio Legislature, a minister, a TV personality, an author and a public speaker, but I've always looked after what I valued most—my mother. What I want for her is one of my dreams, one of my goals.

My life has been a true testament to the power of positive thinking and the infinite human potential. I was born in an abandoned building on a floor in Liberty City, a low-income section of Miami, Florida, and adopted at six weeks of age by Mrs. Mamie Brown, a 38-year-old single woman, cafeteria cook and domestic worker. She had very little education or financial means, but a very big heart and the desire to care for myself and my twin brother. I call myself Mrs. Mamie Brown's Baby Boy and I say that all that I am and all that I ever hoped to be, I owe to my mother.

My determination and persistence in searching for ways to help my mother overcome poverty and developing my philosophy to do whatever it takes to achieve success led me to become a distinguished authority on harnessing human potential and success. That philosophy is best expressed by the following …

"If you want a thing bad enough to go out and fight for it,
to work day and night for it,
to give up your time, your peace and your sleep for it…
if all that you dream and scheme is about it,
and life seems useless and worthless without it…
if you gladly sweat for it and fret for it and plan for it
and lose all your terror of the opposition for it…
if you simply go after that thing you want
with all of your capacity, strength and sagacity,
faith, hope and confidence and stern pertinacity…
if neither cold, poverty, famine, nor gout,
sickness nor pain, of body and brain,
can keep you away from the thing that you want…
if dogged and grim you beseech and beset it,
with the help of God, you will get it!"

Branding Small Business

RAYMOND AARON

Branding is an incredibly important tool for creating and building your business. Large companies have been benefiting from branding ever since people first started selling things to other people. Branding made those businesses big.

If you're a small business owner, you probably imagine that small companies are different and don't need branding as much as large companies do. Not true. The truth is small businesses need branding just as much, if not more, than large companies.

Perhaps you've thought about branding, but assumed you'd need millions of dollars to do it properly, or that branding is just the same thing as marketing. Nothing could be further from the truth.

Marketing is the engine of your company's success. Branding is the fuel in that engine.

In the old days, salespeople were a big part of the selling process. They recommended one product over another and laid out the reasons why it was better. Salespeople had credibility because they knew about all the products, and customers often took the advice they had to offer.

Today, consumers control the buying process. They shop in big box stores, super-sized supermarkets, and over the Internet — where there are no salespeople. Buyers now get online and gather information beforehand. They learn about all the products available and look to see if there really is any difference between them. Consumers also read reviews and check social media to see if both the company and the product are reputable. In other words, they want to know what the brand is all about.

The way of commerce used to be: "Nothing happens till something is sold." Today it's: "Nothing happens till something is branded!"

DEFINING A BRAND

A brand is a proper name that stands for something. It lives in the consumer's mind, has positive or negative characteristics, and invokes a feeling or an image. In short, it's a person's perception of a product or a company.

When all goes well, consumers associate the same characteristics with a brand that the company talks about in its advertising, public relations, marketing and sales materials. Of course, when a product doesn't live up to what the company says about it, the brand gets a bad reputation. On the other hand, if a product or service over-delivers on the promises made, the brand can become a superstar.

RECOGNIZING BRANDING AND ITS CHARACTERISTICS

Branding is the science and art of making something that isn't unique, unique. Branding in the marketplace is the same as branding on a ranch. On a ranch, ranchers use branding to differentiate their cattle from every other rancher's cattle (because all cattle look pretty much the same). In the marketplace, branding is what makes a product stand out in a crowd of similar products. The right branding gets you noticed, remembered and sold — or perhaps I should say bought, because today it is all about buying, not selling.

There are four main characteristics of branding that make it an integral part of the marketing and purchasing process.

1. Branding makes you trustworthy and known

Branding makes a product more special than other products. With branding, a normal, everyday product has a personality, and a first and last name, and people know who you are.

In today's marketplace, most products are, more or less, just like their competition. Toilet paper is toilet paper, milk is milk, and a grocery store by any other name is still a grocery store. However, branding takes a product and makes it unique. For example, high-quality drinking water is available from just about every tap in the Western world and it's free, but people pay good money for it when it comes in a bottle. Branding takes bottled water and makes Evian.

Furthermore, every aspect of your brand gives potential customers a feeling or comfort level that they associate with you. The more powerful and positive that feeling is, the more easily and more frequently they will want to do business with you and, indeed, will do business with you.

2. Branding differentiates you from others

Strong branding makes you better than your competition, and makes your product name memorable and easy to remember. Even if your product is absolutely the same as every other product like it, branding makes it special. Branding makes it the first product a consumer thinks about when deciding to make a purchase.

Branding also makes a product seem popular. Everyone knows about it, which implicitly says people like it. And, if people like it, it must be good.

3. Branding makes you worth more money

The stronger your branding is, the more likely people are willing to spend that little bit extra because they believe you, your product, your service, or your business are worth it. They may say they won't, but they will. They do it all the time.

For example, a one-pound box of Godiva chocolates costs about $40; the same weight of Hershey's Kisses costs about $4. The quality of the chocolate isn't ten times greater. The reason people buy Godiva is that the brand Godiva means "gift" whereas the brand Hershey means "snack". Gifts obviously cost more than snacks.

4. Branding pre-sells your product

In the buying age, people most often make the decision on which products to pick up before they walk into the store. The stronger the branding, the more likely people are to think in terms of your product rather than the product category. For example, people are as likely, maybe even more likely, to add Hellmann's to the shopping list as they are to write down simply mayo. The same is true for soda, ketchup, and many other products with successful, strong branding.

Plus, as soon as a shopper gets to the shelf, branding can provide a quick reminder of what products to grab in a few ways:

- An icon or logo
- A specific color
- An audio icon

BRANDING IN A SMALL BUSINESS

Big companies spend millions of dollars on advertising, marketing, and public relations (PR) to build recognition of a new product name. They get their selling messages out to the public using television, radio, magazines, and the Internet. They can even throw money at damage control when necessary. The strategies for branding are the same in a small business, but the scale, costs, and a few of the tactics change.

Make your brand name work harder

The name of a small business can mean everything in terms of branding. Your brand name needs to work harder for your business than you do. It's the first thing a prospective customer sees, and it is how they will remember you. A brand name has to be memorable when spoken, and focused in its meaning. If the name doesn't represent what consumers believe about a product and the company that makes it, then that brand will fail.

In building your product's reputation and image, less is often significantly more. Make sure the name you choose immediately gives a sense of what you do.

Large corporations have millions of dollars to take a meaningless brand name and make it stand for something. Small businesses don't, so use words that really mean something. Strive for something interesting and be right on point. You don't need to be boring.

Plumbers, for example, would do well setting themselves apart with names like "The On-Time Plumber" or "24/7 Plumbing". The same is true for electricians, IT providers, or even marketing consultants. Plenty of other types of business are so general in nature they just don't work hard enough in a business or product name.

Even the playing field: The Net

The Internet has leveled the playing field for small businesses like nothing else. You can use the Internet in several ways to market your brand:

Website: Developing and maintaining a website is easier than ever. Anyone can find your business regardless of its size.

Social Media: Facebook and Twitter can promote your brand in a cost-effective manner.

BUILDING YOUR BRAND WITH THE BRANDING LADDER

Even if you do everything perfectly the first time (and I don't know anyone who does), branding takes time. How much time isn't just up to you, but you can speed things along by understanding the different levels of branding, as well as the business and marketing strategies that can get you to the top.

Introducing the Branding Ladder

Moving through the levels of branding is like climbing a ladder to the top of the marketplace. The Branding Ladder has five distinct rungs and, unlike stairs, you can't take them two at a time. You have to take them in order, and some businesses spend more time on each rung than others.

You can also think of the Branding Ladder in terms of a scale from zero to ten. Everyone starts at zero. If you properly climb the ladder, you can end up at 12 out of 10. The Branding Ladder below shows a special rung at the top of the ladder that can take your business over the top. The following section explains the Branding Ladder and how your small business can move up it.

THE BRANDING LADDER	
Brand Advocacy	**12/10**
Brand Insistence	**10/10**
Brand Preference	**3/10**
Brand Awareness	**1/10**
Brand Absence	**0/10**

Rung 1: Living in the void

Your business, in fact every business, starts at the bottom rung, which is called brand absence, meaning you have no brand whatsoever except your own name. On a scale of one to ten, brand absence is, of course, zero. That's the worst place to live and obviously the most difficult entrepreneurially. The good news is that the only way is up.

Ninety-seven percent of businesses live on this rung of the Branding Ladder. They earn far less than they want to earn, far less than they should earn, and far less than they would earn if they did exactly the same work under a real brand.

Rung 2: Achieving awareness

Brand awareness is a good first step up the ladder to the second rung. Actually, it's really good, especially because 97 percent of businesses never get there. You want people to be aware of you. When person A speaks to person B and says, "Have you heard of "The 24/7 Plumber?" You want the answer to be "yes".

On that scale of one to ten, however, brand awareness is only a one. It's better than nothing, but not that much better. Although people know of your brand, being aware doesn't mean that they are interested in buying it. Coca Cola drinkers know about Pepsi, but they don't drink it.

Rung 3: Becoming the preferred brand

Getting to the third rung, brand preference, is definitely a real step up. This rung means that people prefer to use your product or service rather than that of your competition. They believe there is a real difference between you and others, and you're their first choice. This rung is a crucial branding stage for parity products, such as bottled water and breakfast cereals, not to mention plumbers, electricians, lawyers, and all the others. Brand preference is clearly better than brand awareness, but it's less than halfway up the ladder.

Car rental companies represent a perfect example of why brand preference may not be enough. When someone lands at an airport and needs to rent a car on the spot, he or she may go straight to the preferred rental counter. If that company has a car available, it's a sale. However, if all the cars for that company have been rented, the person will move to the next rental kiosk without much thought, because one rental car is just as good as another.

Exerting Brand Preference needs to be easy and convenient

If all you have is brand preference, your business is on shaky ground and you can lose business for the feeblest of reasons. Very few people go to a second or third supermarket just to find their favorite brand of bottled water. Similarly, a shopper may prefer one store over another but, if both stores sell the same products, he or she will often go to the closest store even if it is not the better liked one. The reason for staying nearby does not need to be a dramatic one — the shopper may simply be tired, on a tight schedule, or not in the mood to travel.

Rung 4: Making it you and only you

When your customers are so committed to your product or service that they won't accept a substitute, you have reached the fourth rung of the Branding Ladder. All companies strive to reach this place, called brand insistence.

Brand insistence means that someone's experience with a product in terms of performance, durability, customer service, and image has been sufficiently exceptional. As a result, the product has earned an incredible level of loyalty.

If the product isn't available where the customer is, he or she will literally not buy something else. Rather, the person will look for the preferred product elsewhere. Can you imagine what a fabulous place this is for a company to be? Brand insistence is the best of the best, the perfect ten out of ten, the whole ball of wax.

Apple is a perfect example of brand insistence

Apple users don't just think, they know in their heads and hearts, that anything made by Apple is technologically-advanced, user-friendly, and just all-around superior. Committed to everything Apple, Mac users won't even entertain the thought that a PC may have positive attributes.

Apple people love everything about their Macs, iPads, iPhones, the Mac stores and all those apps. When the company introduces a new product, many of its brand-insistent fans actually wait in line overnight to be one of the first to have it. Steve Jobs is one of their idols.

Considering one big potential problem

Unfortunately, you can lose brand insistence much more quickly than you can achieve it. Brand-insistent customers have such high expectations that they can be disillusioned or disappointed by just one bad product experience. You also have to consistently reinforce the positives because insistence can fade over time. Even someone who has bought and re-bought a specific brand of car for the last 20 years can decide it's just time for a change. That's how fickle the world is.

At ten out of ten, brand insistence may seem like the top rung of the ladder, but it's not. One rung is actually better, and it involves getting your brand-insistent customers to keep polishing your brand for you.

Rung 5: Getting customers to do the work for you

Brand advocacy is the highest rung on the ladder. It's better than ten out of ten because you have customers who are so happy with your product that they want everyone to know about it and use it. Think of them as uber-fans. Not only do they recommend you to friends and family, they also practically shout your praises from the rooftops, interrupt conversations among strangers to give their opinion, and tell everyone they meet how fantastic you are. Most companies can only aspire to this level of customer satisfaction. Apple is one of the few large corporations in recent history that has brand advocates all over the world.

- Brand advocacy does the following five extraordinary things for your company. Brand advocacy:
- Provides a level of visibility that you couldn't pay for if you tried. Brand advocates are so enthusiastic they talk about you all the time, and reach people in ways general media and public relations can't. You get great visibility because they make sure people actually listen.
- Delivers free advertising and public relations. Companies love the extra super-positive messaging, all for free.
- Affords a level of credibility that literally can't be bought. Brand advocates are more than just walking testimonials. They are living proof that you are the best.
- Provides pre-sold prospective customers. Advocate recommendations carry so much weight that they are worth much more than plain referrals. They deliver customers ready and committed to purchasing your product or service.

- Increases profits exponentially. Brand advocates are money-making machines for your business because they increase sales and decrease marketing costs.

For these reasons, brand advocacy is 12 out of 10!!

BRANDING YOURSELF: HOW TO DO SO IN FOUR EASY WAYS

If you're interested in branding your product or company, you may not be sure where to begin. The good news: I'm here to help. You can brand in many ways, but here I pare it down to four ways to help you start:

Branding by association

This way involves hanging out with and being seen with people who are very much higher than you in your particular niche.

Branding by achievement

This way repurposes your previous achievements.

Branding by testimonial

This way makes use of the testimonials that you receive but have likely never used.

Branding by WOW

A WOW is the pleasantly unexpected, the equivalent of going the extra mile. The easiest and most certain way to WOW people is to tell them that you've written a book. To discover how you can write a book of own, go to www.BrandingSmallBusinessForDummies.com.

Sex, Love and Relationships

DR. JOHN GRAY

Just as great sex is important to lasting love, good health is important to sex and relationships. About 12 years ago, I cured myself of early stage Parkinson's disease. The doctors were amazed, but my wife was even more amazed. She noted that our relationship and sex life had become dramatically better. It turns out that the natural supplements I used to reverse Parkinson's can also make you more attentive and loving in your relationship. At that point, I realized that good relationship skills alone were not enough to sustain love and passion for a lifetime.

I shared many insights gained from my 40 years' experience as a marriage counselor and coach in *Men Are From Mars, Women Are From Venus*. And while my insights go a long way towards helping men and women understand and support each other, good communication skills alone are not always enough. For better relationships, we not only need to be healthy, but we must also experience optimum brain function.

If you are tired, depressed, anxious, not sleeping well, or in pain, then certainly romantic feelings will become a thing of the past. My recovery from Parkinson's revealed to me the profound connection between the quality of our health and our relationships. This insight has motivated me, over the past twelve years, to research the secrets of optimum health as a foundation for lasting love.

These are health secrets that are generally not explored in medical school. In medical school, doctors are indoctrinated into the culture of examining the symptoms, identifying the sickness, and prescribing a drug to treat that sickness. They learn very little about how to be healthy or to sustain successful relationships.

There are no university courses entitled "Better Nutrition For Better Sex". Drugs sometimes save lives, but they also have negative side effects that do little to preserve the passion in a relationship. Ideally, drugs should be used as a last resort and 90 % of our health plan should be drug free. From this perspective, the heath care crisis, as well as our high rate of divorce in America, is indirectly caused by our dependence on doctors and prescription drugs.

Most people have not even considered that taking prescribed drugs (even for the small stuff) can weaken their relationships, which in turn makes them more vulnerable to more disease. For example, if you are feeling depressed or anxious, a drug may numb your pain, but it does nothing to help you correct the cause of your problem. It can even prevent you from feeling your natural motivation to get the emotional support you need. In a variety of ways, our common health complaints are all expressions of two major conditions: our lack of education to identify and support unmet gender-specific emotional needs; and our lack of education to identify and support unmet gender-specific nutritional needs.

With an understanding of natural solutions that have been around for thousands of years, drugs are not needed to treat many common complaints. Some symptoms like low energy, weight gain, allergies, hormonal imbalance, mood swings, poor sleep, indigestion, lack of focus, ADD and ADHD, procrastination, low motivation, memory loss, decreased libido, PMS, vaginal dryness, muscle and joint pain, or the lack of passion in life and/or our relationships can be treated drug-free. By using drugs (even over-the-counter drugs) to treat these common complaints, our bodies and relationships are weakened, making us more vulnerable to bigger and more costly health challenges like cancer, diabetes, heart disease, auto-immune disease, dementia, and Alzheimer's. In simple terms, by handling the easy stuff (the common complaints) without doctors and drugs, we can protect ourselves from the big stuff (cancer, heart disease, dementia, etc.) We can be healthy and also enjoy lasting love and passion in our personal lives.

Even if you are taking anti-depressants or hormone replacement therapy, sometimes all it takes to stop treating the symptom is to directly handle the cause. With specific mineral orotates (something most people have never heard of) or omega three oil from the brains of salmon, your stress levels immediately drop and you begin to feel happy and in love again.

For every health challenge, we have explored the effects on our relationships, with as well as natural remedies that can sometimes produce immediate positive results. You can find these natural solutions to common health complaints for free at my website: www.MarsVenus.com.

What they don't teach in medical school is how to be healthy and happy without the use of drugs or hormone replacement. By refusing drugs and taking responsibility for your health, a wealth of new possibilities can become available to you. We are designed to be healthy and happy, and it is within our reach if we commit to increasing our knowledge.

New research regarding the brain differences in men and women reveals how specific nutritional supplements, combined with gender-specific relationship and self-nurturing skills, can stimulate the hormones of health, happiness and increased energy. Over the past 10 years in my healing center in California, I witnessed how natural solutions coupled with gender-specific relationship skills could solve our common health complaints without drugs. By addressing these common complaints without prescribed drugs, not only do we feel better, but our relationships have the potential to improve dramatically.

Ultimately the cause of all our common complaints is higher stress levels. Researchers around the world all agree that chronic stress levels in our bodies provide a basis for any and all disease to take hold. An easy and quick solution for lowering our stress reactions is specific nutritional support combined with gender-smart relationship skills. Extra nutritional support is needed because stress depletes the body very quickly of essential nutrients. When a car engine is running more quickly, it uses fuel more quickly. When we are stressed, we need both extra nutrients and extra emotional support. Understanding what we need to take and where to get it requires education. Every week day at www.MarsVenus.com I have a live daily show where I freely answer questions and provide this much-needed new gender-specific insight.

At www.MarsVenus.com, we are happy to share what we have learned for creating healthy bodies and positive relationships. You can find a host of natural solutions for common complaints and feel confident that you have the power to feel fully alive with an abundance of energy and positive feelings that will enrich all your relationships.

Unstoppable

The Art of Striving

DEREK G. CHAN

HOW TO BE UNSTOPPABLE

It has been said that in order to obtain a goal, one must first see it in the mind. The child who decides he wants a cookie from the jar that's high up on the shelf or the person who wants to make partner in the law firm where they now work—each uses the same mechanism or mindset. They understand at a visceral level that you become what you think about.

The difference between the student who can break boards with their hands and feet and the one who can't, isn't skill—it's all mindset, the belief, the deep-seated knowledge that one can do it.

Golf is an interesting game. The person who can best remember the components of a good swing AND can also envision them is the one who will hit the ball far, true and straight. So it is with martial arts: you must develop a set of beliefs or a mindset that will allow you to become unstoppable. Your approach needs to be holistic in nature.

Definition of Holistic: relating to or concerned with wholes or with complete systems rather than with the analysis of, treatment of, or dissection into parts

- Holistic medicine attempts to treat both the mind and the body
- Holistic ecology views humans and the environment as a single system

At Ko Fung Martial Art, we train body, mind and soul, integrating the three elements into a holistic mindset that will make you unstoppable in life.

One of my students, Lesia Rogers, had this to say about our "wellness" approach:

Sifu Derek has truly been a blessing to me, and I am extremely grateful. It has been a year this month since he took me under his wing to teach me how first to love myself. I've also been given many tools through martial art training, coaching and nutrition.

When I first started with Derek, I was already training with someone in Tai Chi, but I'd always wanted to learn self-defence and was looking for a different martial art. Interestingly, the first thing Derek coached me to do was slow down, something I still struggle with to this day.

In the beginning, I was extremely scared and hesitant, but Derek maintained a strong awareness and was always sensitive to my needs. This was important to me as I am an emotional person and needed to reset my mindset to love, acceptance, trust, building confidence and not being afraid of life. He spent hours with me and was by my side through the thick and thin of my life (my accomplishments and my challenges). It has not been an easy journey.

I learned that it takes time for change to happen, that it requires belief in ourselves, and through coaching and training Derek has given me the beautiful gift of awareness of who I really am and what I really want in life. He's made me realize anything is possible if I truly want it. For example, I spent five years with other trainers struggling with little change in my WEIGHT. The first thing Derek did was teach me about mindset to help me understand what it takes to achieve my weight loss goal. By slowing down, listening, AND DOING, I was able to lose 10 pounds in less than two months.

Most recently he has taught me that we often face challenges in life that we have no control over. With the sudden loss of my husband, he has taught me by being there for me that life must go on. In fact, if it wasn't for Derek in the past year, I wouldn't have been prepared to deal with this sudden loss and the corresponding changes in my life.

Change is very scary and can happen suddenly. Although nobody is ever really prepared for tragedy, we must move on and take back control of our lives. Derek has been very supportive and has taught me about acceptance, redirecting and letting go with everything we do in life.

I am a stronger person than I was a year ago when we first started. Thank you to Derek. I know I would be worse off without his coaching.

I had no idea how disciplined martial art can be until I met Derek and learned his way of life. And even though I am now alone (we are never really alone), I am beginning to fill the empty space within by learning to be by myself and love myself truly.

Grateful for every moment and every breath I take, thank you, Sifu Derek.

As mentioned, martial arts represent a pathway to developing a mindset that allows you to be unstoppable. I'll provide a holistic approach to developing this mindset in your own life and give you the tools to deal with hard times whenever you encounter them. You'll learn about martial arts principles and how to apply them to your daily living. Being unstoppable is not about fearlessness or strength, but about recognizing fear and still moving forward.

In training, a martial artist gets used to regular defeats and, in turn, sees them as an opportunity to learn. Tou Lou (martial art routine) or the forms in martial arts teaches us progression. One sequence of movements leads to another. You must learn each fundamental movement first before you can move to the next sequence of movements. This structured type of learning and milestone-based achievement is valuable in all aspects of life.

Wing Chun, in particular, is an effective tool to prepare those who practice it for real life. It does so by developing skills necessary for when one encounters difficult situations. Its concepts and principles are particularly enlightening when properly interpreted and digested under a good Sifu's guidance. Form in the Wing Chun system teaches the practitioner—Awareness, Body Structure, Balance, Body Mechanics and Relaxation. Technique drills or single drills in the Wing Chun system teach the individual how to use those principles during a confrontation.

An essential aspect of having an unstoppable mindset is the ability to make timely decisions in stressful and ambiguous situations. A decision may be either right or wrong, but it's crucial to remember that far worse than an incorrect decision is a situation where no decision is made when one is necessary. Through a variety of cooperative and semi-cooperative drills, a Wing Chun practitioner is able to develop intuition, reflexes and decision-making skills while under pressure.

An example of a Wing Chun drill that develops these skills is the famous 'Chi Sao' (sticking hand) training. It is a two-person tactile sensitivity drill. One only does the attacking while the other is only defending. The objective of the attacker is learning how to use leverage, distance, angle and openings to create a successful attack. At the same time, the defender is learning how to maintain proper body structure, relaxation and counter movements while under pressure with unplanned attacks. The key to Chi Sao is accepting the force coming in (relaxation) instead of using force against force.

This develops decision-making skills through checking assumptions against facts, and develops problem-solving skills by making its practitioners consider the possible impact of their decisions throughout the process of the drill. This gives the two practitioners an opportunity to test their strengths and weakness while promoting unique and unplanned learning processes to occur.

POWER OF BREATH - STRESS MANAGEMENT

A crucial concept in Wing Chun is that of proper breathing. Siu Nim Tao is the first open hand form from the Wing Chun system and is a form of breathing meditation. Siu Nim Tao translates to "Little Idea," meaning everything starts with a thought. Without proper breathing, movement becomes stilted and ineffective. Proper abdominal breathing is a skill that is crucial for a healthier and stronger body and also for focus, which is why it is one of the first things taught.

In addition to the health and training benefits of breathing, it can also be used as an important tool for stress management. Breathing has both voluntary and involuntary control mechanisms. You can shift from being its pilot to allowing it to be left on autopilot. The voluntary aspect of breathing is what allows us to tap into its stress-managing potential.

Breathing exercises act as a form of meditation in Chinese Martial Arts. Proper abdominal breathing used in this type of meditation allows a greater volume of breath and leads to a decrease in activity of stress markers and blood levels of stress hormones.

Oftentimes, when our life is stressed, the integrity of our automatic breathing suffers. Taking advantage of the control we can exert on breathing allows us to combat stress. Learning to control our breathing can allow us to begin to control other parts of our body as well. The mind-body connection developed through breathing exercises not only physically improves our breathing but can also increase self-awareness. When you bring your body and mind in tune, your mental state will be much improved, and less susceptible to stress.

BODY STRUCTURE

Martial arts teach the skills of how to use your body structure to your advantage, and offers understanding on how the body's structure works in terms of structural alignment, the linkage of the joints, and also how simple geometry and physics can be applied to the body. A central focus of Wing Chun is adopting particular stances and postures as a framework from which to launch attacks and counter-attacks. Doing this without good posture will greatly limit your ability to be effective. In fact, your Wing Chun techniques won't be as effective unless your body is aligned correctly. This alignment also reinforces the important concept of breathing and can directly impact your ability to draw and use your breath.

Good posture means that the body is aligned with gravity, walks tall and moves with freedom in the joints. Posture in martial arts is vitally important.

This is the reason most martial arts emphasize structure from the beginning. Physical structure from a Kung Fu point of view involves a little more than just good posture, though. In addition to good posture, it adds internal connections such that your entire body learns to move as a single fluid and powerful unit.

The efficient way to get a feel for a student's structure is through single drills, Chi Sao and sparring. Good structure can be almost invisible—even to the trained eye. However, the lack of it can usually be felt as soon as contact is made with your opponent. If an opponent has good structure, a lot of techniques you could try are unlikely to work, but if their structure is poor or non-existent, almost anything you do will be effective.

What exactly is good structure and why is it so important? To put it in simple terms, good structure is the way in which you connect the different parts of yourself together internally so that they are aligned with the forces acting on your body. In Wing Chun principle and theory, the curves of the spine should be aligned, eliminating as much curvature as much as possible. It's done by tucking in the chin backward and slightly scooping forward the tailbone to avoid an anterior pelvic title. Shoulders should be relaxed and dropping with the body. By doing so, the body is able to absorb and deliver a force as one bodily unit.

The majority of people are completely disconnected and don't have proper alignment and coordination with their body. Their arms will do one thing, their legs something different, with hips only being vaguely involved. When the body does so many different things, it's impossible to connect the breath or the mind to what it's doing. This results in internal chaos and a feeling that you lack the resources to cope with your physical situation. The truth is, you don't lack the resources at all; you've just scattered them. The key to good structure is in learning how to gather all the parts of yourself together so that you can put everything you are into everything you do.

Good structure connects your arms and legs together through your centre and involves your breath working in harmony with your movements. Most importantly, the whole process is controlled by your mind, which stays focused on what you're doing. When you're connected internally, every movement involves your whole body. This internal structure can easily be felt. For example, when you try to move someone's arm who is well connected internally, you can feel that in trying to move their arm you are moving the weight of their whole body.

RELAXATION

Relaxation is a great example taught in martial arts that can easily be applied to everyday life. To be relaxed is to be natural. It should be like pouring water into your cup without any muscle tension. To get a better understanding of how to apply this in daily life, we remember how relaxation, in the context of martial arts, is supposed to be understood.

When I teach Wing Chun, I like to begin by emphasizing to my students that, in training, techniques are performed in a relaxed manner. This occurs both during training and in actual combat. In order to develop force, one must be able to relax. Why? The equation for force is mass multiplied by acceleration, and if there's any sort of muscle tension, it will only slow down the acceleration. I tend to use an analogy of a car. In order for a car to move smoothly, you will have to step on the accelerator. Step on the brake and accelerator at the same time, and it will feel like you're getting a lot of power, but in reality, you're not going anywhere.

If the arm is tensed, maximum punching speed cannot be achieved. To begin a punching motion, the arm must, in essence, first be relaxed. If relaxed at the onset, the punching may begin at any time. It is a fact that one motion is always faster than two. If there is unnecessary tension, energy will be wasted, and this will, in turn, create fatigue. In an extended engagement, this can be critical. Tension stiffens your body and thus reduces your ability to sense and react to your opponent's intentions. Look at the sport of boxing. The best boxers don't get tired—even after 12 rounds. A huge part of this is that they don't waste energy on inefficient movement. Less experienced boxers may look good early in a fight, but they often crumble in the later rounds due to not being relaxed.

I will now paraphrase two of the core points of this lesson:

1. **Tense muscle slows down your reaction speed.**
2. **Unnecessary tension wastes energy, causing fatigue.**

If you're overcome by anger or are tense, your mind faces identical effects and, consequently, you'll have difficulty acting with the speed you need. This unnecessary tension in your mind doesn't only waste your energy and time, it also creates a lot of undesired situations that will now need to be solved. A person with a relaxed mind can always see things more clearly than a quick-tempered person. Thus, they can easily react with proper speed and attitude. This is why a person who understands the principle of relaxation correctly can certainly be more careful and successful; they react only when necessary by keeping calm and relaxed.

BALANCE

Balance is important to all martial arts, and especially Wing Chun. It's a concept that ties together both relaxation and structure. Without balance you can't maintain structure, nor can you be relaxed as you'll always be fighting to adjust yourself and the structure you've moved away from.

The Merriam-Webster dictionary defines balance as follows:

bal·ance noun \ba-lən(t)s

- The state of having your weight spread equally so that you do not fall
- The ability to move or to remain in a position without losing control or falling
- A state in which different things occur in equal or proper amounts or have an equal or proper amount of importance

Balance in Kung Fu is often associated with the physical sense of the word. I teach my students from the day they walk in how to understand their bodies in order to develop the balance necessary to perform the forms and techniques in Wing Chun. However, physical balance isn't the only form of balance a martial arts student should learn to hone. Balance in Wing Chun isn't only about your own physical body, but understanding how to create balance between two individuals. The highest level in the art of Wing Chun isn't about how to destroy or how to inflict the most pain in an individual, but how to neutralize and balance an opponent's incoming force without harming them, and at the same time preventing them from hurting you.

"The best battle is the one that has not been fought."

- Sun Tzu

This is one of the other reasons why in Wing Chun we'll focus heavily on Chi-Sao, as it helps us understand how to find balance between two individuals—either by changing to a different position or stepping in a different angle. This is one of the skills that's transferable to everyday life and relationship-building.

There is a saying that Wing Chun Kung Fu is easy to learn but hard to master. One reason is that, in the Wing Chun system, there's a fine balance between each movement and technique. Each movement needs to be precise. There can't be any gray area as it could be a matter of your life or death in a physical confrontation. In order to find the fine balance, though, one must understand not what to do but what not to do.

Understanding this concept will also help you find balance with your overall well-being and health. It's not about knowing what type of workout we should be doing or what type of food we should eat, but what we should not be doing or eating on a daily basis. Example: all rigorous physical activity can wear down the body, and you can feel tired, sore or injured. One must always balance training and rest, and in the case of an injury, you must listen to your body. Training when too fatigued or coming back too soon from an injury can set your training back by keeping you out even more in the long run.

ROOTING AND CENTRALIZATION

"When you have roots there is no reason to fear the wind."
- Chinese Proverb

In order to understand how to become unstoppable in classical martial arts training you must recognize that it all begins with the foundation. So what does the foundation include? Strengthening the lower body by lowering your center of gravity and widening up your base. Learning how to align your skeletal structure at the same time as relaxing your body. If we're able to be rooted to the ground and our body is up straight, it's most likely going to be harder to be pushed out of balance. You can try this when you are taking the bus or subway.

1. **Imagine your head is being slightly pulled up.**
2. **Widen your base (knees are a shoulder width apart).**
3. **Slightly bend your knees to lower your center of gravity.**

You'll automatically feel more balanced and centered. A solid base is required in order for you to grow your skills and techniques. It's the same in life. It's important to understand what keeps you grounded, to discover both your values and your beliefs. By doing so, you're able to hold your ground no matter what conditions life gives you.

By being grounded, you'll eliminate fear and find inner peace. This happens as you gain the courage and strength to overcome whatever fears you might have. Training in the martial arts will always push you to your limits. It tests not only your physical strength but your mental strength as well. Know this: each time you're ready to give up, you're facing a true test of willpower. You push yourself to the limit to see how much more you can take and to see how much more you're willing to go through in order to achieve your goal. This mental strength develops into an unbreakable warrior spirit, giving you the courage to persevere through your darkest hours.

ACCEPTANCE AND LETTING GO

At a certain point in your training the ability to 'let go' becomes essential. The concept of letting go functions on two levels—physical and mental. To be able to truly let go, the physical, mental (includes emotional) aspects must function in unison.

Physically you learn to relax and release your muscles, tendons and ligaments. When you do this, it leads to the deepening of one's root and the ability to ground a powerful incoming force. In terms of meditation, this means relaxing as much as possible and 'trusting' the Earth to hold you up.

The emotional and mental aspects of 'letting go' are intertwined, meaning that emotions can trigger thought patterns, and certain thought patterns can trigger emotions. You should look for evenness and balance in your emotion. This is a non-reactive state rather than an absence of emotion per se. This emotional neutrality is like a placid lake that appears to be a mirror. In this state, it becomes possible to read a person's true emotional intention like an open book.

For the mind, you want, at first, a gentle calmness and a slowing of thought, but this eventually develops into what has been termed 'mind of no mind.' This mind of no mind is actually an optimal state for both the meditative aspect as well as the martial. For meditation, we can perceive and become aware of things without the mind's judgement. In martial arts, this 'mind of no mind' state is optimal for success in combat. When centered in such a state you are able to act or react at a speed that can be faster than the speed of thought!

Accepting and letting go are probably two of the hardest things to do. Whether it's a relationship, anger from an argument or simply past mistakes; instead of being stuck in the moment, accept the emotion and the situation with your arms wide open. Acknowledge, embrace and let go. Let go of emotions and situations that don't serve you as a whole or lead you to greater things. It's beyond whether you were right or wrong. It's about setting yourself free. It begins with the willingness to accept ourselves exactly as we are, right where we are, with no judgements or preconceived notions. For the martial element, you must go even further. Instead of fearing an opponent's attack, you must learn to welcome it. This is all a matter of lack of tension. Therefore, the stronger an attack, the more relaxed you must initially become to deal with it. This method is grounded in a Wing Chun principle that states, "Accept what comes, escort what leaves." By accepting the incoming force, it will enable you to reposition and let go of what's coming in at you.

Once this is accomplished you no longer react to circumstances as average people do. Instead, you find yourself centered and alert—ready to deal with a situation without having your natural adrenal reaction getting in the way. This is not only supremely useful in combat but also in your daily life.

MOVING FORWARD

"Your one-step back is your opponent's two-step forward."
–Derek G. Chan

One of the most important rules of Wing Chun is that you don't step back. It is structure that gives us the advantage over the larger opponent, and when we become our worst enemy by destroying our own structure, it's not too difficult to predict the outcome of a fight. While Wing Chun may have backward stepping and backward bracing, these footworks are not designed for you to initiate. In Wing Chun we always move forward; only when the force dictates it do we actually move backwards. Footwork in Wing Chun is always taking you forward. It might be in a direct straight line or at an angle, but it allows you to swallow up any space that opens up between you and an attacker, limiting their options and overwhelming them.

Some of the most skilful boxers are those that can deliver a knockout blow while going backwards. While this may be much to the appreciation of the crowd, Wing Chun has no time for any of this. The footwork drives you forward all the time. One of the most important rules I always remind my students of during our sparring sessions is to continue to move forward—mentally and physically. It's important to create opportunities either by footwork, by stepping in a different angle, or a follow-up technique. There may be times when it is best to be stationary and wait for the perfect timing and openings. However, if you are against a more experienced opponent, the only chance of you overcoming the situation is by closing the distance and creating the opening. If you don't, not only do you have a lesser chance of winning, you're also leaving yourself vulnerable as a stationary target.

By having the attitude of forward movement, it will greatly benefit you in your daily life. Life is your experienced and stronger opponent. It doesn't matter how organized or how well-planned you are; life will always throw obstacles at you. In order for you to conquer them, you must start by moving forward. If you keep waiting for the perfect time or the perfect day, you'll never get anything done, and, sadly, you'll also miss a lot of opportunities. Instead, start moving forward and create your own path, regardless of how tough the situation is. If there's a will there is a way.

FOCUS

It can take a continuous daily effort to reach your goals. However, focusing on your long-term expectations, you'll find the strength to keep going even in the face of temporary setbacks. Those trained in Wing Chun will tell you that in the process you'll face a lot of challenges and setbacks. The students who are able to recognize that such setbacks are necessary hurdles and pitfalls they must navigate along the path to their destination are also the ones who succeed. Without that realization a student faces great difficulty overcoming those setbacks because they may lose sight of their long-term goals and allow themselves to get lost, joining the many casualties who fall by the wayside.

To focus, you must not only find a goal but also envision and look beyond at what lies ahead. The same principle applies to Karate practitioners when they attempt to break boards. If they only focus on the surface, their success rate of breaking the boards decreases as their force will be slowed down before they reach the target. However, if they are envisioning and telling themselves to hit behind or through the boards, the chance of them breaking the board is a lot higher.

Life is a series of experiences. There will be times where you're stuck in the moment. Whether it's a failure in a business partnership or the loss of a family member, it's up to you to endure and envision what lies ahead and continue to march forward. By doing so, you'll develop a stronger self and character. This is what separates those who are short-sighted from those who are long-sighted.

TECHNIQUE—EFFICIENT AND ECONOMICAL

"Offence is Defence, Defence is Offence."
- Wing Chun Proverb

One of Wing Chun's unique points is that it doesn't rely on any brute strength to overcome an adversary. We'll always place ourselves as the fragile person. Why? There will always be someone bigger, stronger and faster. And the way to overcome a larger assailant is by understanding the power of proper body structure and relaxation.

To become more efficient and economical with your movements, you'll defend and attack simultaneously. Doing so will allow you to become more efficient with your movements. One example is the Lap Da or Lap Sao technique. This is a technique where one hand sinks the opponent's straight attack while your other hand punches. In order to execute these fine movements, there will be an emphasis on body coordination drills. Without being coordinated, you wouldn't have the ability to execute the technique as smoothly. Wing Chun techniques often require you to have your hands and lower body cooperating with one another. Being well coordinated also means one is well-balanced. As human beings, we already apply the principle of balance while we are walking, our left hand will swing out, right foot steps forward, and vice versa. However, as a martial artist sometimes we tend to forget about this basic principle, and we think martial arts movements and everyday movements are two separate entities.

Having the Wing Chun mindset of being efficient will change our approach to handling daily tasks. It will help us realize how important it is to utilize our energy more efficiently (as it will help us manage time). In Wing Chun philosophy, time is an important factor. For this reason, each movement and technique has to be precise. As it could be a matter of life or death if you're in a confrontation. Every inch, every angle, every movement comes into play. Wing Chun is a system that does not discriminate, as it is not about who is bigger, stronger and faster. It's about understanding how to utilize proper body mechanics and physics to your advantage. It's understanding how to execute the most impactful thing efficiently and effectively in the limited time and energy you're given. This is why, in classical martial arts, you'll strike on vital spots and soft tissues on the opponent when placed in a life or death situation. By embracing this Wing Chun concept, you're able to focus more and utilize your time and energy more efficiently and effectively in your regular daily routine.

To learn more about Derek's method of Wing Chun visit us at
www.kofung.ca or contact us at info@kofung.ca

Project Management

How to be Extremely Efficient and Remain Profitable While Developing Any Project

GUSTAVO A. VALENZUELA

The Project Management Institute (PMI) officially defines project management as the application of knowledge, skills, tools and techniques to project activities to meet the project requirements.

To properly manage any project, you must have acquired, through actual management experience, specific knowledge pertinent to the needs of the project. Furthermore, as a project manager, you must have skills in negotiation, decision making, trust building, crisis management, conflict management and verbal and oral communication. These skills and more are needed to remain in control of the entire project's team and their performance. However, being able to visualize and fully understand the project as a whole is probably the best ability you can have and is necessary in order to know immediately, at any phase and at any given time, if the project is moving forward in the best possible way.

LOPPM (LACK OF PROPER PROJECT MANAGEMENT)

In many situations, project owners without a project manager can only appreciate the services of a seasoned project manager when the project is in crisis and they are desperately seeking help. This is not an unusual situation, as people will often take on projects without fully understanding what they are getting into. They'll sign the contract, then get slammed by the intricacies of the project. and the many requirements and processes they must follow, without realizing that an experienced project manager is the ideal person capable of delivering the project within scope, schedule and budget.

While working closely with project owners, I concentrate on increasing their involvement in the entire project development. As a result, they're thrilled to feel in control of their project, especially their budget. They truly appreciate having my experience and expert advice as I act as their project manager. If you would like to benefit from the services of an experienced project manager, please visit www.TheBookonPM.com

WHO RUNS PROJECT MANAGEMENT?

You, as the hired project manager, are responsible for running all such entities, while also keeping in mind that stakeholders may influence your process, something that deserves to be seen as an opportunity for you to remain in control of managing the project—as long as you hold them accountable and make them aware that budget, project schedule and scope may be affected by their requests and attempts to run your project.

WHAT IS AND WHAT IS NOT PROJECT MANAGEMENT?

Initially, your main goal is to select the most effective and ideal team that will run itself without micro or macro managing every aspect and assigned task. If you're successful and your budget can afford to assemble a team of experts, the project will most likely run smoothly (as long as you're able to properly manage it). Having the best team doesn't mean you can stop acting as the project manager. You must also watch all aspects and processes; the scope, compliance, the budget and the schedule. Allowing things to happen and disconnecting your management eye from a project because you've established trust and confidence in the team's abilities isn't really considered project management.

Even when you have the best team to develop your project, a successful project manager is always looking for opportunities to improve the process, to save money, to be more efficient and perhaps even to discover new ways to improve the bottom line. There are opportunities with every project to adjust, improve and even systemize processes to become more efficient, to stay engaged throughout the entire process and to capitalize on those opportunities. By performing your duties as a project manager at all times, your expertise and level of confidence will be elevated and will rightfully separate you from amateur project managers seeking to complete a project just as required.

When you ask yourself "What is Project Management?" you may now add, "The ability to remain connected and engaged throughout the entire process in order to positively affect scope, budget and schedule."

A ROBUST DEFINITION FOR PROJECT MANAGEMENT

As you work in project management, you'll realize the importance of taking your duty as a project manager beyond your contractual agreement. You are already expected to apply your knowledge, your skills and your techniques to meet the project requirements. But by choice, you must make it a personal practice to consciously look for the greatest benefit for the project regardless of what is in your project manager contract.

Project management is inclusive of moral values for both personnel and stakeholders, project managers must also have proper understanding while managing diverse personalities, cultural differences and beliefs. Your decision to go beyond management of project scope, budget, schedule, risk, quality and resources sets you apart from the herd.

How will you know when you are going the extra mile? When you come to that situation in which you tell yourself "This is outside my contractual duties," but you're certain that if properly addressed and handled it will positively influence the outcome of the project—and you simply choose to do it.

To download guidelines on effective steps and ideas on how you may push yourself to consistently go the extra mile, please visit www.TheBookonPM.com

Last, in a new definition of project management, you could easily add, "The ability to include everything tied to any project and place it under the responsibility of a qualified project manager who's able to handle whatever arises, always taking action for the benefit of the project." That would be an all-inclusive contract only a few project managers would confidently sign. If you include yourself in that list of the selected few that would sign such a contract, you are a project manager at heart.

WHY PROJECT MANAGEMENT?

Anyone with the financial means to do so can develop an intent to manage a project without the proper knowledge and specific experience. However, the results will not be favorable for any of the variables that matter, such as scope, budget and schedule. The truth is they will lose money—in the millions—as a result of their innocence and obvious unsophistication in the subject. In the United States, around 68% of the projects fail in at least one of the three critical areas and 98% of those failed projects lacked the services of a project manager. Even more revealing, the remaining 32% of the projects that did not fail were properly organized and managed by an experienced workforce and included the services of an experienced project manager. More so, for every billion invested in the United States, $122 million is wasted due to lack of project performance and proper management. Even more shocking, the failure rate is 50% higher for projects with budgets over $1 million. In most cases, the project owner doesn't even know they are losing money or that they are overspending.

Next time you are acting as a project sponsor or if you are the actual project owner, realize that you may not have the correct talent in your organization to properly develop a project. Additionally, make the right choice and wisely avoid assigning your project and its management to an inexperienced workforce.

EFFECTS OF HAVING AN EXPERIENCED PROJECT MANAGER

The simplest way of saying this is that having an experienced project manager in your development team managing every aspect of your project is the equivalent of having a cardiovascular surgeon perform open heart surgery on you rather than the Chief Executive Officer (CEO) of the hospital. Only project managers can do the job of a project manager, despite the common belief that anybody in the team can wear multiple hats and perform several duties. The effects of having an experienced project manager will indeed be favorable and noticeable, always revolving around success.

LOSING CONTROL AND MONEY

The margin for keeping or losing control of your project is very narrow. There are a number of factors that can be directly related to losing control of your project. Scope creep, departing staff, wrong skill sets being allocated to the project ad lack of focus from the project team can all lead to disaster and you losing control of the project.

Managing tasks, keeping an open communication line with your active team members and setting the stage for upcoming team members are all good practices for staying in control. Many outside factors may also cause you to lose control of the project and if that is the case, your immediate attention is required. Take a step back and reassess the situation as a whole. Once you've gained complete understanding and a clear picture, you may develop a plan to begin turning the project around and back on track. As soon as you identify and begin to tackle a challenge, you have begun gaining control of the project.

Losing money in a project is often tied to key pieces of information being excluded or overpriced by vendors and which are crucial for a successful project completion. You must also have a well-developed ability to review and negotiate bids, quotes or any costs associated with the project. Hence, it is vital that a project manager has the project owner first review the entire project scope and then approve all proposed costs for the correct and just amount of money. Project owners tend to ignore these critical initial operations. At the end, this translates to loss of revenue via wasteful unnecessary spending to the point that your project is not fully completed or ready for occupancy.

To download guidelines and a checklist on effective steps you may take to avoid or stop losing control and money, please visit www.TheBookonPM.com

ACCOUNTABILITY OF STAKEHOLDERS

As a project manager, you're required and expected to execute processes and move through project phases in a clear way so that the planning and approving process for scope is definitive and formal, as to avoid and minimize changes. Hence, when any stakeholder—including the project owner or sponsor—requests a change in scope, budget or schedule you can hold them accountable for what they've requested. People, in general, change their minds constantly and if you're one of those project managers who make challenging and impossible projects seem easy because of your expertise, organizational skills and outstanding people skills, owners will feel invited to propose changes anytime they feel like it. There's a lot at stake and it's your duty to communicate and paint a clear picture for all stakeholders. Formally and officially remind the project owner about the process for approval of scope then pull out and present their approval document with their signed name, signature and date. Point out the paragraph addressing "changes in scope" in which, in sum, it communicates that after approval, and especially during the middle of production, any changes in scope will drastically and most definitely affect budget and schedule. If the owner is still adamant about his request, prepare the correct documents and amend the project's budget to properly compensate your team for accommodating such a late request.

HOW MANY PHASES ARE FOUND IN PROJECT MANAGEMENT?

As a project manager you'll go through the basic phases in any of the projects you're managing. These phases may include: initiating, planning, execution/ production, monitoring/controlling and closing or close out phase. These are the general overall main phases or, in simple terms, the summary of the whole picture.

As a project manager, it is advantageous if you choose to see subphases within major phases. A phase is simply a grouped set of goals or requirements containing a number of steps. Once completed in the allocated time, that phase has been attained and the project can progress to the next phase. So, it's for your own benefit, as you become an extraordinary project manager, to identify what those subphases are in your project.

By breaking down a phase into subphases or a major set of goals into individual goals, you have created a daily, weekly or monthly to-do list to execute your job as an effective project manager. Moving from goal to goal or from point A to point B has new meaning. This simple technique will allow you to visualize and understand the whole picture of any project and at the same time, it will allow you to see and understand the smallest detail of the project.

WHEN TO ENGAGE A PROJECT MANAGER

As a project owner or sponsor, as soon as you get an idea to develop a project, call a project manager and hire him to assist and represent you in the entire process. Nonetheless, at any phase of the project a seasoned project manager can keep things clear, honest and legal. A project manager can hold everybody accountable and in strict compliance with their contractual obligations, on behalf of the project owner and in consideration of established goals of the project. The earlier a project manager is engaged, the more beneficial it is for stakeholders and the project variables, including scope, budget and schedule.

To hire and benefit from having the expert advice of a project manager in your organization, please visit www.TheBookonPM.com

EFFICIENCY DEFINITION THROUGH A PROJECT MANAGER'S LENS

Improving your abilities and skills to manage scope, time, quality, costs and risks logically and habitually happens after you completely understand projects as a whole and after having the benefit of actually managing several projects from start to end and beyond

Only when choosing to know all the project details and team requirements is efficiency born. Then you as the project manager acting as a project leader and working closely with stakeholders can define critical project milestones. Having open communication allows you as the project manager to attain pertinent documentation required to easily move the project forward. Equally as important, understanding and managing risks on a daily basis and taking corrective action will drastically improve overall efficiency.

HOW TO GET AN "A-TEAM"

The success of your project is based in great part on the quality of experience of your selected team members. Therefore, during team selection, first seek for relevant, proven and verifiable experience that is as close as possible to the requirements of your project type. Second, look for people with strong abilities to solve problems and verify they have the right knowledge and access to tools to tackle the most complex challenges the project may face. Third, evaluate their longevity and stability in the specific tasks they're working on. Last, ask them to enlist their strengths and explain why they're interested in becoming part of your team. Always check the validity of all information as submitted and do verify their references.

After accomplishing full compliance with the project's legal requirements, you may assist the procurement team with verifying the project's technical and special requirements. Intentionally choose a diverse selection committee with specific expertise in different areas of the development, including scope, execution, finance, policy, technical, maintenance, warranty, life cycle, or other areas identified as important to the specifics of the project.

Once you have performed all these duties, you ought to consider receiving from all vendors a formal statement or summary of qualifications (SOQ) as part of the documenting process. Gather, review and rank all information, and then interview the top five vendors.

To download a smart list of SOQ items, please visit www.TheBookonPM.com

THE RIGHT INTERVIEW QUESTIONS

Efficient project management is directly related to efficient use of time and opportunities. Utilize the interview to ask only questions that will give you a new insight into the vendor's knowledge, expertise or specific skills. Also, use the interview time to ask the tough questions vendors are not usually asked.

When submitting a written SOQ, the vendor has all the time in the world to formulate a written answer. However, during an interview the vendor only has seconds or minutes to formulate and give his response. As a result, his response is real and it informs you how this particular vendor will handle things during the development process. It's easy for a vendor to state in writing that they have years of experience and can handle your project, but during the interview, if you formulate real questions based on actual project requirements, you'll be able to tell if that vendor is truly knowledgeable and has the right procedures and tools to move the project forward.

Ask questions about all critical areas of the process, including, initiation, planning, execution, monitoring and controlling, closing out, warranty, operational phase and sustainability. This line of questioning truly filters vendors. Those with real, honest experience are able and willing to share their answers in great detail. Then, verify their response by calling their references.

To rely on the expert advice of a project manager to guide your team during vendor interviews, please visit www.TheBookonPM.com

EFFICIENT WAYS TO GET YOUR PROJECT DONE

After you wisely organize processes and all project tasks are properly delegated, you must concentrate on maximally producing or realizing tasks on that specific day; Verify that critical tasks' requirements are clearly identified, that the required work for execution has been delegated to the right party. Then verify the project is performed as planned. Always be two steps or more ahead of your own schedule. Before, during and even after project development, continuously ask yourself "How can I be more efficient?" Any and all ideas that come to mind, simply try them out. If they're successful, choose to make them part of your process on all your future projects.

ORGANIZATION BASED ON EFFICIENCY AND FLOW

The number of people and tasks required to properly and successfully complete a complex project is immense. Subsequently, intending to keep track of them all in your mind is not an efficient way to get your project done. A single organizational chart depicting names, assigned tasks (below stakeholder's titles) and properly organized by the project's phases allows for an efficient way to channel information for proper review and approval. Indeed, an entire project's directory is an important document to keep updated for the benefit of effective project management. Relying on a complete organizational chart is a clear way to see the entire picture, including the review and approval process for each of the project phases.

Organizational charts with detailed information regarding the review and approval process can show the flow of important information either up or down. Up information may include items such as change order requests, payment application requests or allowance use authorizations. Down flow information may include an instance when an owner requested a change in scope, a failed inspection report or a corrective action plan. If an owner sees graphically, in an organizational chart, how many people he's affecting with his "simple request to change scope" he or she may reconsider his request.

Use a detailed organizational chart as a tool for stakeholders to realize the importance of understand positioning and flow in the project's team. As a result, this will create continuity and efficiency.

RECOGNIZE THE ACTUAL STATUS OF YOUR PROJECT

As you create your progress summary report, make a commitment to be completely honest as you report on scope, budget, timeline, risks, quality and percentage completed. Sometimes owners get feedback from other sources and honesty will be your best practice if it comes down to verifying the validity of your report. Reporting on all areas of the project helps your efficiency and saves time as you avoid having several separate meetings.

If the project risk is high on any project area, formulate potential solutions on how to mitigate or eliminate such risks. Any solutions you present ideally you've already discussed with your team prior to presenting them to the project owner. It's important to report on key areas without inundating stakeholders with too much information, especially if it is technical information.

Staying in control of the project also allows stakeholders to sense and see that the project is in great hands and that you are on top of things and two steps ahead.

MONOTONY = BORED DISCONNECTED TEAM

It's true that repetition makes you better at anything, however, during project development, a lack of variety and interest paired with a tedious routine may affect the moral and emotional well-being of your team. Anytime you have a team who is bored working on your project, you're close to having a team that is disconnected from your project. After disconnect comes inefficiency and inevitable mistakes or inaccuracy with scope compliance.

There are many ways you can avoid monotony or promote variability. One way is to allow your team members to fully understand the project's mission and not just the task at hand. You may choose to reward an early finish and accuracy as a way to keep the team excited about accelerating their portion of the work and being accurate and in full compliance with scope.

You may also share some exciting news about the project such as plans to submit for a worldwide recognition award or being acknowledged on important social media sites as a way to recognize them for their portion of the work. The main idea is to avoid monotony and make your team feel appreciated. You want to periodically remind them that their portion of the project is just as important and meaningful as the rest.

For other great ideas on how to keep your team motivated, please visit www.TheBookonPM.com and download a complete list of ideas and techniques, which will keep your team energized and connected to your project.

SYSTEMIZING THE PROCESS

Ideally, your system model wisely accommodates individual expression. This means that as long as the team's creative choices during execution yield the established and required system results, team members can decide how and in what ways their execution may be more fun, efficient and varied. The goal of having a system is to create organization and improve predictability. Furthermore, a system allows for new team members to enter the system and become productive in the least amount of time possible.

Having expert skills and knowledge in a particular field drastically increases your accuracy when completing a specialized task. For instance, you may recognize that your expertise in project management is what gives value to your daily work and your brand. Likewise, recognizing your team's individual expertise will allow you to properly delegate tasks and increase accuracy to the point of achieving perfection.

ELEMENTS OF A GREAT SCHEDULE

A schedule is basically WHAT needs to done, by WHEN and WHO is responsible for it. The project schedule is also required to comply with contractual milestones and it must be formulated with the level of detail required by the contract.

Schedules can serve as a daily, weekly and monthly guide and they're a reliable tool to verify estimated versus actual progress for the completed portion of the project. The level of detail or task description in a schedule varies depending on whom the schedule is written for and what the true intent is for having it.

You may also consider adding enough information to allow listed tasks to act like a to-do list. In fact, including critical reviews and approvals and listing an inspector's information may be extremely practical and beneficial. Adding the sequence for review and approval and listing appointed personnel to perform such duties will be a great way to organize and make the entire team aware of critical inspection events.

Note: Every time you catch yourself thinking "I need to remind myself to do this," and that specific task is not on the schedule, simply add it and test if having such information listed is beneficial to the entire team.

LOOK FURTHER INTO CRITICAL TASKS

Is it possible to dig deeper into critical tasks and find information worth sharing on the project schedule? Absolutely! If you further investigate and understand who is at the bottom of any task or performing any type of work, including review or approval, then adding their information to the schedule will provide you with another level of management. Make a practice to identify every single person involved in any of the processes. By doing so, you'll be able to expedite compliance with that specific task.

FACTORS SHAPING YOUR SCHEDULE

There are other factors shaping or affecting a project's schedule and knowing these factors exist helps the team to plan and allocate time just in case they arrive. Although some of these factors impacting your project schedule, such as climate and accidents, are completely outside your control, you may still formulate a plan to mitigate their effects on your schedule. In the case of climate, knowing climate trends and identifying rainy seasons can help you plan for such an event.

Other factors difficult to plan or accommodate in your schedule include sick people, new hires, new trends, changes in scope, additional safety, omissions, new regulations, unforeseen conditions, etc. You, as the project manager working with your team, may formulate and agree on a plan of action to take if any of the previous factors happen to arrive during your project. Having an agreed plan of attack drastically reduces downtime and excuses for not having a potential solution in place.

HOW TO ADDRESS UNFORESEEN CONDITIONS

In every project, unforeseen conditions and events arrive and test your skills and ability to find solutions. There are some basic steps you must take in order to address unforeseen conditions. First, immediately attend to it by identifying who's in charge of that specific portion of the project. Secondly, once you identify the appropriate party, perform an internal "911" or urgent phone call to the individual in charge to explain the emergency and the urgency for them to address the issue at hand immediately. Third, look at your schedule for float and identify items you may borrow time from to address the unforeseen condition. Then take necessary measures to resolve the issue effectively. Last, choose to plan ahead of time for unforeseen conditions by creating an allowance in your budget for such situations. One of the main reasons unforeseen conditions do not get immediately attended is because there are no funds allocated to pay for the required resources to solve the matter at hand.

Follow the steps listed above on every project you manage and you'll certainly handle any unforeseen condition as a true professional in charge of managing the entire project development.

To benefit from the expert advice of a project manager, to receive assistance reviewing your project's documents or to identify potential unforeseen conditions prior to officially starting your project, please visit www.TheBookonPM.com

WHAT CREATES UNWANTED CHALLENGES IN A PROJECT

Unwanted challenges are often created by unrealistic owner expectations with scope, budget or schedule. Also, inadequate project funding and an inexperienced owner or stakeholder making critical project decisions will always result in an undesirable turn of events. It's common to invite unwanted challenges as early as when procuring and selecting a team if selection is solely based on costs instead of experience or expertise. Even as you review and approve their contracts, having insufficient contractual responsibilities will invite your team and project to face unwanted challenges. As a project manager, the inability to exercise stakeholder accountability may also bring unnecessary, challenging situations to the project. Once unwanted challenges arrive, the project may enter into crisis.

THE CRISIS MANAGER

If you're ever invited to handle a project in crisis, it's a clear sign that you've gained the respect and trust from the project owner, a sponsor or your employer. If you're a great, experienced project manager, you probably have gained the respect and trust from all three entities already. Project managers who can see the big picture and understand every phase and every single detail of the complete development of a project can in fact and will certainly jump on the opportunity to take over a project in crisis. It's like a doctor performing surgery on a patient diagnosed as inoperable or incurable. The doctor goes in with all he's got and does what he does best and cures a patient deemed incurable.

Once assigned to handle a project in crisis you must assume the responsibility of solving any and all project issues and challenges without assigning blame. It's the professional and right thing to do. Let attorneys do their job, when their services are engaged. Managing a project in crisis is about finding solutions and implementing the best solutions to gain control of the project and by having a clear mission to get it back on track. Your immediate goal ought to be to do whatever it takes to guide it and manage it to a successful completion.

When you act as a crisis manager it's a perfect opportunity to display your knowledge, expertise and acquired specialized management abilities. If, on the other hand, you're a project owner or a sponsor, keep in mind that one sure way to get your entire team and your project into a crisis is to choose to develop a project without the services of an experienced project manager.

AM I TO SAVE, FIX OR PULL THE PLUG?

There are instances in which the only option is to terminate a project. The most obvious reason is when financial resources have been exhausted and there's no money to save, fix or complete a project. Also, anytime a project is affecting and endangering public safety, you must consider ending such a project. The main reason project management takes place is precisely so that the project gets completed. Salvaged projects brought to completion help stakeholders and they also help you become a better project manager. Therefore, work to rescue a project before you come to the conclusion to terminate it. Your final recommendation to stakeholders must be a professionally written statement listing your precise reasons for why the project is to be salvaged or terminated.

DEFINITION OF A SUCCESSFUL PROJECT

Is a pleased project owner enough of a reason to consider the project a success? Of course, it's not. If you hit the targets defined in your scope and the project is in absolute compliance with your budget and schedule, then you may correctly state that you have completed a successful project.

Relying on successful values, such as honesty, confidence, perseverance, integrity, innovation and adaptability, provides a solid base for success to rest upon. Celebrating your victories and embracing your challenges helps you learn and become better. These are also crucial factors to be included in your ever-changing formula for success.

Write your own definition of success and share it with the rest of the project's team. It will provide a clear target and allow for recognition and celebration when the team hits the bull's eye and the project's purpose is accomplished. Watch for the team and stakeholders saying "WOW" and use that as an indicator that success is surely on its way.

To create "WOW" experiences on all your projects, and to learn how the proper management techniques will create the "wow" factor everywhere, please visit www. TheBookonPM.com

PROJECT DELIVERY WITH A MISSION

Knowing the specific purpose for developing a project allows project management to revolve around a clear mission. A project manager who's aware of the main project's mission and understands the "What," "Why," and "Who" can easily focus resources around these reasons.

Make it part of your own personal practice to ask the project owner or sponsor, why this project? And do ask about the mission or main purpose for developing this project.

PROJECT MANAGEMENT BENEFITS YOUR BUSINESS PROFITABILITY

Learning to delegate responsibilities is an ability you develop once you fully comprehend, through extensive experience, what people can do for you and the project. Project managers are experts in understanding what each team member is responsible for and what each is capable of contributing to the progress and completion of the project.

Inexperienced project owners tend to delegate tasks to the inappropriate person or party. For example, they ask engineers questions meant for architects and ask architects to attend issues meant for a general contractor. During project management, simple mistakes cost money—a lot of money.

Money allows the project to start, then project management allows the project to move forward and, last, it allows for the completion of the project. It's a fact that money is truly the heart of the project and without it, the project may not survive. As you become more efficient and knowledgeable about reviewing and approving costs, your ability to reduce overspending by millions of dollars will increase. It will also allow your project management skills to benefit any organization financially.

To increase your business's bottom line and maximize profit, please visit www. TheBookonPM.com and schedule a professional consultation with an experienced project manager.

EVERY PROJECT IS UNIQUELY DIFFERENT

Even if you work in franchise project development and every project has the exact same requirements and goals, so they all look the same, the simple fact that the project is in a different location will make that project uniquely different. It's true, no two projects are alike, and as you recognize that every project has a unique set of rules and variables you'll begin to adapt to properly managing the differences in your projects.

Project management expands across several industries and is a profession practiced worldwide. Since scope for projects are diverse, procurement and team members are also diverse. It's like a meal using the exact same ingredients but cooked by different chefs; the taste and even the way the meal is served on the plate will be different. Subsequently, it's a smart practice to systemize your processes used during the project development to become more efficient and to allow repetition of tasks, so the parts of your process become automatic and predictable. In a way, the variables and differences in a project are what makes project management enjoyable. And, truthfully, your ability to handle the differences in diverse projects is what makes you a unique project manager.

A MEASURING STICK

How do you measure your project's success? There are many indicators to tell you that your project is going well and that you're being successful. For instance, a happy owner who's recommending you to other clients to the point that he already sold your services is a great sign that you're on the right track. Perhaps success shows up as passing every inspection with flying colors and earning the respect of inspectors. But for many people who trade their talent and time for money, the ultimate indicator for success comes via a significant bonus at the end of the year. You may have all or some of the previously mentioned indicators, but other important factors may not be present, such as the emotional well-being of the entire team. Moreover, there may be vendors who feel they were strategically obligated to do things outside their contract just to gain the opportunity to do business in future projects.

When half of the indicators aren't present and you receive an award, how would you feel about being recognized? On the other hand, if all indicators are there and no award is given, you'll probably feel blissful and accomplished.

It's nearly impossible to measure the true success of a project. You can't expect everybody to be completely satisfied, fully pleased and always preferring you as their project manager. Having stated this, how about outlining, during the planning process and scope definition, what would be considered a success for the project you're managing? This may give you a clear target that's easy to identify and a set of guidelines and expectations regarding the positive outcome of the project. Ask for and document a definition for success for your project in your detailed scope, vision, mission or your "goals documents." Then, work to get there.

CLOSE OUT

It's time to finalize all project activities and verify everything is completed across all phases. As you enter this phase and close the project to transfer the completed project as required the end of the road for the majority of your team members is near. You, as the project manager, have some critical and important steps to take before you sign off on the closing of all phases. During this phase it's critical to involve all project participants and stakeholders and use a robust checklist to make sure you cover each and every item that has been completed.

Soliciting feedback as you conduct a post-project survey is more opportunity to understand how the entire team feels about the project as a whole and in specific areas outlined in your survey. Including a "lessons learned" meeting allows you to gather useful information for the benefit and success of future projects. During this phase the collecting of project data to be archived is the actual deadline for the majority of the team members. If your project requires archives to comply with any regulations such as NARA (US National Archives and Records Administration) or others, verify that all submitted documents and data are in full compliance.

The checklist pertaining to your close out procedure may be extensive as every project has its own unique requirements and stakeholders often require specific information, such as financial audits. They may also have confidentiality requirements and may require disposal of sensitive information in order to properly close out a project. Ideally, your checklist for the close out phase is amended with every project you manage and it's your practice to always include a formal meeting with stakeholders prior to arriving at this particular phase.

USEFUL LIFE COSTS

For many developments, project management ends at the completion of a project, once the owner takes full control of the completed product. Infrequently, the project manager participates in managing the warranty period, typically lasting up to two years. Depending on the project delivery method, you may be asked to remain in the project since you are the official holder of the information pertaining to just about everything regarding the completed project.

If you're given the opportunity to participate in the management of a completed project, such as a building, while occupied by its end users you will get to see its operations and experience the maintenance phase. Thus, your ability to see the whole picture and have a better watchful eye during production will get sharper—since you'll have important knowledge about why things fail and need to be repaired during the two-year occupancy period (in the case of a building).

Always make the owner aware of the importance of performing a life cycle cost analysis, which simply means a complete understanding of total costs of ownership. Having the financial means to develop a project until the point of making it functional and operational is considered by most a healthy project budget. Eventually, the daily operational costs requirements of the building begin along with its demands for repairs and replacements. Often keeping up with expenses becomes such a big challenge that businesses are closed, buildings are abandoned or their functionality is limited.

To benefit from the services of an experienced project manager, please visit www.TheBookonPM.com and schedule a professional consultation.

SUSTAINABILITY

How long can anything be maintained at a certain rate or level? Even more specific, how long can a project sustain its healthy life while serving its intended function? And last, for how many years can it be sustained without undesirably impacting its surroundings or the environment?

The UN World Commission on Environment and Development definition for sustainability reads: "Sustainable development is development that meets the needs of the present without compromising the ability of future generations to meet their own needs." Now, since buildings require money to stay alive, let's look at financial sustainability. Imagine two people are sitting side by side and each of them have one dollar. The only way these two people may remain side-by-side is to give a dollar and then receive a dollar. So person "A" gives a dollar to person "B" at the same time person "B" gives a dollar to person "A" This process, as long as it happens precisely as described, can be sustained indefinitely. When there are multiple streams of income, including sophisticated systems for income generation coupled with a sound administration for all finances, your odds for remaining sustainable just increased.

Every project is to include the commonly avoided sustainability conversation since many project owners usually ignore it. Carefully bring this subject up and address its requirements. Working closely with all stakeholders, do your best to utilize the entire team's abilities. If you must, hire expert advice.

DECODE, DECRYPT AND DECIPHER

Documenting the entire process and creating a reliable system to access it, read it and understand it, may be one of the major challenges the project development industry faces. The information produced before, during and after a project in development is vast as it's inclusive of everything in relation to the entire life cycle of that project.

The main purpose for documenting a project is to have the ability to understand how, what, who, when and why things were developed in a certain way. There are many processes to organize, archive and access information, however no software out in the market does it all. Hence, you may be required to provide a hybrid solution to comply with project archiving and retrieval.

Make it a practice to document project information in a clear way so that

30 years from today, anybody who accesses the project database will be able to fully understand it.

A FINAL NOTE

Now, give yourself credit. Your project management knowledge, skills and tools have been complemented just by the mere fact you have read this book. Your journey as a project manager will be filled with amazing opportunities to leave this world a better place. Your participation in project management along with millions of fellow project managers around the globe will add to the efforts of the fastest growing profession in the world. Be efficient, honest and stay true to your values. Surprise yourself first, and every project you manage will become successful in every way, just as you imagined it. Share your story; spread the joy and your knowledge to those around you. You're already an amazing project manager. All that's left to do is for you to let it come out.

It is time to play! Enjoy your journey, as you may now efficiently and profitably perform project management.

Above and Beyond

DR. MARYLYN POYNTER

"Retirement at sixty-five is ridiculous.
When I was sixty-five I still had pimples."

- George Burns

When I hit retirement, I honestly thought that life would be amazing. I had spent many years as a dental surgeon and now I was looking forward to enjoying life, my way.

At first, my retirement fund seemed fine but a few years in I realised that my pension was not allowing me to live the life I dreamed. I had wanted to do things with my husband, but I also had kids and grandkids that I wanted to do things for and support.

I felt frustrated and trapped. What was I going to do? Go back to work? I had already spent a lifetime working. This was supposed to be the time for me to do what I wanted. The other option was to continue as I was, always juggling my wants and needs. Not being able to live my dream and leave money for the future generations.

Neither one appealed to me.

Do you feel that way? Like you have no choice but to accept the way your retirement is going and hope that there may be something left over when you pass?

What if there were other options? What if you had a choice? What if you could set goals and reach them? That is what we are going to explore in this chapter. Many retirees I have talked to are living lives of quiet desperation when they don't have to.

I decided to do something about my situation and researched my options. Can I admit something to you? It was pretty daunting. What could a woman of my age do? Going back to school to learn a new trade was not feasible, plus, who would want to?

I could get a part-time retail job but to me that seemed like moving backwards after all my years of being an educated professional. Plus, I valued my free time, and there was a golf course with my name on it.

What else could I do? Then an idea came to me. I googled it and my first thought was, "Maybe." I always try to keep an open mind and be courageous enough to try new things.

Want to know what it was? I was considering running an online business. Are you shocked? I was, and I was the one considering it.

Have you considered working online and then came up with all the reasons why you can't?

Do any of these reasons sound familiar to you……

1. Too Old to Learn the Technology

Aren't computers, websites, and online shopping for young people? There is no way you can learn those things They are way beyond your skills. You will look so foolish. People will laugh at you and think you are stupid for even wanting to try.

2. Isn't it Expensive

By the time you get everything set up, isn't it going to cost a lot of money? How do you know that you will get that money back? You have some money, but you can't afford to lose it. How long will it be before you are making money? These are all questions people ask themselves.

3. What to Choose

If you google, "How to make money online?" the options are endless. How do you choose? Which ones are scams and which ones are shiny objects that distract you from your true course. All these questions need to be answered.

But for me, learning how to do things online was different. I have always been one who sees the goalpost, moves towards it and just as I reach it, move it back. I want my life to be one of forward motion where I am always learning and growing. So, I chose to do something most people my age wouldn't even consider; I started learning how to set up a business online.

Was it easy? No. Did I require help? Yes. Did I make mistakes and get caught up in shiny object syndrome? Yes. Yes. Yes. I spent money on trainings and programs that were a distraction, but almost two years later I am making five figures, travelling, enjoying time with my family, and partaking regularly in my favourite hobby, golf. Life is good.

How was I able to do that? I put aside my doubts and my pride and I learned how. I tried new things, asked for help, and spent a lot of time on YouTube (what an amazing website, you can learn anything you want on there for free,). I outsourced some things and, most importantly, I got the professional coaching, training, and support that I needed to succeed.

MY CHALLENGE TO YOU

You have a choice. You can continue to live the rest of your life struggling financially, not being able to live a full, fun life. You can watch each day go by wishing and hoping that things were different, looking at your kids and grandkids knowing that there is nothing that you can do to help them.

Or…

You can take my challenge and become an online entrepreneur. Now is the time to silent those voices in your head that are giving you all the reasons why you can't succeed. We grew up in a generation where we were taught to be average, to do what everyone else was doing and not to expect anything more.

We were conditioned not to take risks because they might backfire, and people might think we are strange. We can't have that, now can we?

> *"The biggest risk is not taking any risk... In a world that is changing really quickly, the only strategy that is guaranteed to fail is not taking risks."*
> — Mark Zuckerberg

It is time for something new. What if I could show you a way to earn money online? Would you want to learn more? Of course, you would. Here's the thing. If I can do it, so can you. I didn't start this process with great computer skills. I could do the basics but beyond that it was all a mystery to me.

When it comes to learning how to run an online business you have three options:

1. Figure it All Out Yourself

This is how I started. It is the hardest way to go. I spent hours upon hours in the beginning just trying to figure out what business I wanted to do. Then I tried to learn the basics, but it was hard. Easy terms that young people know and understand were like a foreign language to me.

Google and YouTube became my new best friends, but it was such a long process to do the simplest things. There were times I was so frustrated and wanted to quit. Thankfully, I didn't.

I also invested in a lot of training programs that promised the moon and the stars but never delivered. I was excited each time because I was sure that this one would work. I invested time in studying it only to realize that it was just another shiny object, all brilliance and no substance.

So, can you learn by yourself, yes you can. However, although there were many things I learned to do myself, the process was long and tedious, and during that time I wasn't making any money. Which leads to option two.

2. Paying Someone Else to Do It

There are three problems with this solution. First of all, to do everything you need, it is costly. If you don't have a lot of disposable income at hand you will either get very low-quality work or you will have to save between each step.

Second, trying to find honest freelancers who produce quality work and truly care about your project is hard. Sometimes, you go through and pay two to three people before you find a good freelancer and that is wasted money. Third, if you don't know what you are doing, every time you need to make a change you will have to pay someone to do it.

So, if you have the money, this is an option for you (provided you have the time and patience to build a good team of people to help you).

3. Work with a Professional Coach and a System

In my opinion, this is your best option as it incorporates the other two. A professional coach will be able to identify your strengths and weaknesses quickly and guide you to the best resources available to build the business that you want.

A professional coach knows all the ins and outs of running a business online and can help you both avoid the pitfalls and take advantage of the secret loopholes to success.

Their goal is to help you reach YOUR goals and YOUR dreams. What could be better than that? Someone who is on your side and can show you the ropes, will be there when you get discouraged (because you will), and help you navigate the big, wide, online world.

I am going to share a secret with you. I have found a professional coaching system that is economical (under $100USD), gives you a simple 21 step program that is easy to implement, and, on top of that, assigns you your own personal coach who is there to help you each step of the way. (http://marylynsblog.com/something-new.)

I also have some other resources that can help you in your journey to creating an online business. Check out this free PDF I created to help you with your first steps: http://marylynsblog.com/perfect-retirement

Plus, I also have my blog, marylynsblog.com, where you can find lots of free training.

I encourage you to take charge of yourself. Create the business that gives you the freedom to live the life you want and to be a blessing to your family.

I am so glad that I chose to try and didn't give up until I figured it out and now I want to help others do the same.

In closing, remember what Walt Disney said, *"All our dreams can come true, if you have the courage to pursue them."*

For FREE training go to www.marylynsblog.com

Romancing Your Way Through Network Marketing

DORCAS TAY

"By three methods we may learn wisdom: first, by reflection, which is noblest; second, by imitation, which is easiest; and third by experience, which is the bitterest."

– Confucius

I started out in network marketing the way 99% of people do, with no clue what I was doing and no one to show me how. My results proved it. It was hard because I had this desire to make it big but lacked the knowledge and skills to make it work. I was determined to succeed but did not know how to get there.

I spent the next few years going from company to company hoping that each one would be THE ONE. If you have been in network marketing, you know exactly what I am talking about. You always think that the next company will be the magic one that takes you from zero to millions.

Throughout those years there was always one thing I did, and that was learning. I took advantage of every training session I could go to. I read books and watched videos. I devoured anything I could get my hands on.

As time went by something happened, I started to realize that the issue was not with the company, the products, the compensation plan, the team or the prospects. The problem was deep inside of me. I had spent years learning the skills I needed, but at the core of me, I did not honestly believe that I could be successful. I was blocking my goals and dreams from becoming a reality.

If you are reading this chapter, you are probably hoping for some magical revelation or formula that will guarantee instant success. But life does not work that way. There is no gidget, gadget or gizmo that is going to propel you to immediate results.

What I learned during that process changed me forever, and I am so thankful for it. I had self-limiting beliefs, and I was sabotaging myself at every step, subconsciously turning my beliefs into reality. This may sound strange to you, but it is true. No matter how big your desire is on the outside, if your subconscious has been conditioned to believe that you are not worth success, you will unconsciously do things to make what you believe reality and blame everything but yourself. You will block your own success.

Once I figured out what those beliefs were and changed my thinking, life started to become better. I immersed myself in changing those beliefs by attending numerous seminars, workshops, and personal development programmes. Indeed, investing in one's education and growth is wise and has a long-lasting impact on one's life.

From every failure, I learned precious lessons and so can you. If you feel like you are failing, do not nurse the guilt, embarrassment or blame. You can turn the failure into a learning experience.

Avoid blaming others or yourself. Doing so is like falling into quicksand. It will only entangle you deeper into emotional turmoil. The situation will become more complicated, and nothing good will be gained. Spend quiet time in retrospection, evaluate what happened, and embark on an action plan for how to perform better in the next opportunity.

Going through such a process is a necessary path of learning from failure and then trying again. Continually ask yourself, "What can be done differently in the next attempt?" and "Who can I learn from to do this better?" If you are not willing to evaluate and learn from past failures, then all those past experiences are a wasted journey.

WHAT I LEARNED IN NETWORK MARKETING

Over the years I have realized that being in network marketing is a lot like being in a relationship. When you understand all the stages, it will help you to get more results.

The first stage in network marketing is prospecting, which is akin to the dating stage. At this initial stage, you get to know the person who recruited you and the company they work for just like the first dates of a boy and a girl where they get to know each other. Both sides want to make the best impression on the other.

Prospecting is like the first attempt in dating. There is an air of curiosity and anticipation. The excitement is felt more in the first few dates. Thoughts of, "Oh, will Amy be the one for me? Will she be the girl of my dreams?" They flood the mind, and you get butterflies in your stomach.

This is very much the same when a new network marketer meets their first few prospects. Thoughts of, "Oh, will Amy be my downline? Will she be the ace in my team and bring in a lot of people?"

Everyone hopes to meet the ideal downline who will carry the baton, run the race and fight the good fight to the top. Ideally, when this happens, one can then relax and enjoy the sun and sea while passive income keeps flowing in. This is idealistic thinking.

Network marketing does not work this way, as many network marketers would like to have you believe. If you are hoping to meet your ace among your prospects, you are very likely chasing the Holy Grail. To be successful in network marketing, you had better first BE that ace and show the way through your actions and leadership. Just as a dating couple is wishing the other person is the ideal partner, one has to look inward and BE the ideal partner first.

Build genuine relationships with your prospects. Do not just recruit them and then leave the person to fend for him or herself.

As appalling as it is for a person to be used and then left to nurse their hurt and find their own recovery, so it is for someone to be brought into a network marketing company and then abandoned. In such a situation, people do feel betrayed, sore and regretful especially when personal savings were put into joining the network company. To truly build a team, one must diligently ensure the new downline completes the company's business training.

The important part at this stage is clear communication. You may want things from your leader and company that they cannot give, and they may want you to produce more results than you are capable of.

It is essential to let your leader know what you need and then listen and take what you can. Not all leaders are strong, and you may have to accept the fact that you will have to go other places for training. This is your business, and it is your responsibility - both for its growth and your personal success, not the success of others.

The next stage in network marketing is akin to a couple living together. Network marketers share the dream of financial and time freedom. They build the business together, spend time together at trainings, business presentations, and team bonding events. Leaders share a genuine interest in their downline's well-being and success. They work together as a team to achieve their objectives.

This is similar to couples living together, caring for each other, spending time together, and engaging and sharing common activities (meals, household chores, sports, charity work, etc.)

There are network marketers who neglect to build their new downline's knowledge about the products, the company, and the compensation plan. After signing up a new person, the network marketer simply leaves the new joiners to themselves or refers them to call the company's customer care hotline should they have any questions or difficulties.

The network marketer goes on to his next prospect, too busy to spend time with his team's downlines. The new joiner, meanwhile, feels frustrated, abandoned, taken advantage of by the upline. This can be paralleled to an absent father or mother in a family where the kids and household matters are left to one partner. The other partner is too busy at work, or with other activities, to spend time with the family. As we know, such behavior can adversely affect the spouse and children in the long term.

If you want to build strong customers, team members, and businesses, then you must put time into the relationships; you must nurture them. For customers this means providing good customer service, taking care of their needs, providing product information and caring about them.

For your team members, you must spend time with them and train them. You may not know all the answers yet but be there for them. When you do not know the answer, find out for them. Encourage them to come to company events and training. Give them recognition, whether verbally, socially or in the form of prizes. Let them know that they are valued, and they will want to stay with you and build their business.

It is easy at this stage to think that you do not need to give them any attention since they are already 'living with you.' This is the most important stage because the initial excitement has worn off and this is when the true commitment begins.

You are married. Now what?

This is the stage where things start to grow because the level of commitment is there and established. You have developed a good, strong customer base of people who order regularly, and you have built a stable team who want to work. Life gets easy or so you think. While things are easier when you reach this stage, it is tempting to start neglecting everything because you have already made it. Why bother when everything is running smoothly? Like a marriage, if you neglect your marriage, it will decay over time, and eventually, you will not have a marriage anymore.

If you want to stay successful, you must continue to do the things that you did when growing your business. You must be involved and help others to grow too. Continuously give encouragement, rewards and recognition. If you continue to do these things, your business will flourish.

A marriage also produces children, so make babies and more babies! Isn't it exciting how overjoyed a couple feels when they have a baby (particularly the first child)? The happiness even outflows to relatives and friends.

It is the same in network marketing when you have your first sign-up. You are elated as are your uplines and those supportive of your business. However, just as a baby needs to be nourished and nurtured, so does each and every one of your downlines. Just as responsible parenting is crucial for every child's development so is the training and development of your team members in network marketing.

Divorce

Sometimes, you join a company and it is just not the right fit. Maybe you have no support whatsoever from your leader, or even worse, they are making things difficult for you.

Maybe you realize that you cannot support the products with your full heart and they do not give the promised results. Or perhaps you poured out all your effort, passion and belief in the company and products but the company becomes tardy in payment or even stops paying as they should. No matter what the reason, there are times when you need to leave a company.

My suggestion is, if this is your situation, then you need to leave peaceably. Let people know why you are leaving, however, do it in such a way that you keep the relationship in good standing. You never know when that relationship will help you in the future.

What is next? Some people may choose not to stay in network marketing. Maybe they are too hurt or found it too hard.

But…

If your desire is to truly build an amazing business, then you need to find a new company. Take your time and do your research. You have experience now and can make a better decision.

One thing that can never be in network marketing is fear. In the same way that fear will kill a relationship, it will also bring death to your business. Yes it can be hard, especially if you have been burnt before, but each company and leader are different. You have to give them the benefit of the doubt when joining.

Talk to people in the company. Find out who you want to be your leader. Find out about their events and go to them. See what the company is like before you join.

Is network marketing worth it? Of course it is. Perhaps, like me, you may have tried network marketing with little or no success and instead ended up spending money on the products. However, I did enjoy the events and getting to know more people.

Like any other business, you have to invest time and energy for a period of time to bring it to where you want it to be. It is a journey that will not only grow you as a person but will also enrich your life. In some unseen way, all these experiences have helped you become a wiser and more fulfilled you.

The following are tips to help you with your network marketing business. I call them the 12 C's of Network Marketing.

Compatibility. Get to know the person who is recruiting you and find out whether both of you can work well together (know who you are going to bed with). Do not simply join anyone who buys you a coffee (you are not so cheap).

Commitment. Look for people with whom you want to build a long-lasting relationship (enter into a marriage) and who will not just recruit and disappear (have a fling).

Camaraderie. Work together with a passionate force to achieve common goals, no matter what (stick through thick and thin in a relationship).

Communication, Compliments, and Complaints. Take time to know your prospect (know your life partner). Serve each other (a loving husband and wife relationship).

Consideration and Compassion. Do not look at every person you see on the street or anywhere as a prospect (not every person you meet will be desirous to go to bed with you).

Confidence and Ceaseless Passion. Commit your time, energy and effort to grow the size of your team (every new addition of a baby into the family brings great joy and fulfilment).

Celebrations. Create memories of happy times by celebrating achievements, special occasions and holidays (a couple's relationship is strengthened as they spend special happy moments and occasions together).

Charity. Do deeds of charity and incorporate social responsibility as a team to create more bonding, fulfilment, fun, and meaning while earning money (a couple is more fulfilled while looking beyond themselves to serve others in the community).

You can succeed in network marketing if you are willing to put in the time and effort and become the LEADER you want others to be to you.

If you have enjoyed reading this Chapter, do pass it on to someone you know who will also benefit from it.

I encourage you to continually seek learning and improving yourself in whatever you are focusing on. You can only become better.

In my book "LEARN AND BE ENRICHED. CREATE YOUR LIFE THROUGH LIFELONG LEARNING", I share personal life stories with powerful messages that will move you to be more, experience more and contribute more.

My book is available on www.amazon.com and www.dorcastay.com.

Are you curious to know what business I am up to now? Simply drop an email to dorcas.tay@gmail.com or go to www.dorcastay.com and grab your bonus gift today!

Buy Your Neighbour's House

The #1 Real Estate Strategy to Develop Wealth on Your Own Street

BRIAN KLODT

Get rich with the secret goldmine that lives next door!

Have you been searching for a way to improve your financial outlook? Are you worried about having enough money in your retirement years? Are you living the life you want? Do you know what would have the biggest impact on your financial future?

In this chapter, I explain why buying investment real estate, and specifically why buying your neighbour's house (or a house on your street or in your neighbourhood), is a desirable way to develop your wealth, support you in your quest to live a good life and help fund you in your retirement years. Your neighbour's "house" could also be a condominium, townhouse or another type of residential property. I will explain in detail the reasons for doing so along with helpful information on how to go about doing it. Real Estate is one of the best vehicles for the average family to develop long-term wealth and transform financial health.

MY STORY

My story begins in 1989 at the age of 28 years old when, at the peak of the Canadian real estate market, I purchased my first house. It was an existing duplex, a two and one-half story Victorian brick house in a low-income neighbourhood. I bought it for $150,000. Although hindsight is 20/20, looking back I purchased a house doing everything wrong. I bought a good house in a poor location and purchased it at the worst possible time. The conventional wisdom is that you should buy the worst house on the street in the best location. I did the exact opposite. The house came with an existing tenant in the second-floor apartment. The house also had a large unfinished basement. A friend built a basement apartment for me (with some of my limited experience help), and I then had a triplex. After living on the main floor for one year, my fiancé moved into the basement apartment, and we worked to complete the finishing touches there for one more year. In 1991 we were married, and we both moved from our respective apartments to the second-floor apartment, where we fixed up that unit and continued to live there for our first year of marriage. After the third year living in our triplex, we decided to move back to my hometown, about 20 minutes away. It was in an up and coming downtown neighbourhood on a picturesque street, just a few blocks up from Lake Ontario and two beautiful parks. We were able to keep our triplex, because of the good income coming from the three units, there was enough money to pay for all our expenses. It also provided an additional cash flow to put into the bank for all the improvements the house would need. I continued to manage many tenants over the 25 years we owned this house, selling in 2014 for $340,000.

In our second house in the neighbouring city, we began to raise our family in what was just a small 950 square-foot Victorian century home. Our children were born in 1994 and 1998. We had outgrown the house with the birth of our second child, but we loved the neighbourhood location so much we continued to live in the house. We hired an architect to design an addition for our home with the thought we would make the house bigger to live in, but in 2003 the house next door came up for sale. The house was very similar except that it had a large addition in the rear which resulted in a large three-bedroom house. Since we had been receiving income from the triplex for all those years it was a natural thought to purchase our neighbour's house and rent out the house we had been living in. The house was more than double the price we paid for our first house. We asked our friends and family to help us move all our possessions 30 feet south to the house next door, without the need to rent a truck or moving company. We loved transitioning into this larger house, which was in an even better location, being one home closer to the lake.

In 2005, the third of what was only four houses on our block came up for sale. Already owning two of the four houses on the same street, it was again natural for us to think about purchasing the third house. I had set a goal at age 30 to become a millionaire and real estate was becoming our main method for the achievement of this goal. In this case, the market was hot again, and we knew that we would need to act quickly. The night the house came up for sale, we approached the seller's real estate agent directly about purchasing the house. There was going to be another offer made on the property even though the house had just come up for sale. To ensure we were successful with our offer, we proposed $2,000 more than the asking price and became the proud owners of the third of four houses on our street. This house was being used by the prior owner as a hair salon and had been set up to be very eclectic in terms of paint colours (gold crown moulding, orange walls) and kitchen finishing. The kitchen cupboard doors actually had colourful gems and decorative colours affixed to them. We renovated this house and turned it into a rental unit.

In 2006, the owner of the remaining house on the street approached us and asked if we would be interested in purchasing their house should they ever decide to sell. Six months later, at Christmas time, they left a note on our door saying they wanted to talk to us. It turns out they had an opportunity to move out west and were looking to see if we wanted to buy their house. With a loan from my parents for the down payment, we were able to purchase the fourth house on the block. We now owned an entire street of four heritage century homes, all built in the late 1800's, three of them protected with heritage designation. It was difficult to decide whether to stay in our second house or move to this fourth house. The decision to move once again was made due to the larger lot, a wood burning fireplace in the living room, and granite counters in an updated kitchen. The trade-off was that the house was only about 1,200 square feet, smaller than the second house we had lived in. Regardless, we loved this new house. Our children had now lived in three consecutive houses all on the same street.

In 2017, our real estate story of owning all four houses on the street was featured in a real estate investment club's newsletter and we were honoured as members of the month. I was asked to speak at one of their member events on how we were able to accomplish this, and about the unique rental strategy we developed along the way, which you'll read about shortly.

WHY INVESTMENT REAL ESTATE?

Of all the investment classes, real estate is the foundation of a large percentage of high net worth individuals. Since there is only a limited supply of land, and the population of the world continues to increase at record pace, real estate will continue to increase in price when viewed as a long-term investment. There are several unique advantages to owning investment real estate:

- Real estate is something the average person can understand
- You can invest in real estate while having a full-time career and treat it as your "side hustle" or hobby
- You can rent out your real estate and have tenants pay off your debt
- Over time, you can raise the price of your rent to improve your positive cash flow. Positive cash flow means that you'll have money left over after paying for all of the expenses associated with owning the property. When tenants change over, rents can be adjusted to the going market rate. Mortgage payment remains constant, depending on your mortgage term and prevailing interest rates.
- By buying property in "up and coming" neighbourhoods, you can multiply your equity and cash flow gains as the desirability of living in your neighbourhood increases. Equity is the part of the house that you own versus the part the bank owns. Equity is based on the current market value of the house minus the amount remaining on your mortgage.

- Through leverage, you gain the benefits, over time, of controlling a very large asset and the gains associated with it, with a much smaller down payment. As an example, you may only put a 10% down payment to purchase a house which is worth ten times more than your down payment. The gains you make, however, relate to the full value of the house purchase, not just your 10% down payment. As a very simple example using easy round numbers, let's say you put 10% down to purchase a $100,000 house, or $10,000. If your house appreciates 5% in one year, your $100,000 house will be worth $105,000. You've made a gain of $5,000 on your $10,000 investment ($105,000 minus $100,000), which represents a 50% gain ($5,000 gain / $10,000 down payment). This illustrates the remarkable concept and benefit of leverage.

- You can increase the value of your real estate through your own "sweat equity," in which you make your own improvements instead of paying someone else. Sweat equity is a term for using your own physical labour (where you just might get sweaty), resulting in an increase in the value or equity portion of your house because of the improvements. An example would be removing carpeting on your own and installing laminate or hardwood flooring in its place, increasing the value of your house by $10,000. However, you only spent $5,000 on the flooring and materials.

Some people strive to become millionaires to support their retirement goals. Investing in real estate for the long-term is a proven way to become a millionaire. As a continuation of our simple example, let's say you purchase a single-family house for $100,000 which produces a break-even cash flow. After having your tenants pay off your mortgage over 25 years, you'll own the house outright, but after 25 years, the house is likely to be worth at least double what you paid for it. At 5% appreciation per year (quite possible in some locations and markets), your $100,000 house will be worth more than $300,000. Depending on the actual home purchase price, it is possible your house will be worth more than $1,000,000. If your house doesn't appreciate significantly, that's okay too. You'll still have a substantially paid off asset when you're ready for retirement.

As discussed in "my story," in 1992 my wife Kathy and I purchased our first house in my hometown which we lived in for 11 years. We then purchased our neighbour's houses in 2003, 2005 and 2006. We did this while continuing to own and rent the triplex house we purchased in 1989. All of these subsequent house purchases have more than tripled in value since time of purchase. We have developed and been blessed with high net worth and cash flow as a result of investment in real estate, and it has allowed us to live our dream life. Net worth is the resulting value of all the things you own (your assets), minus the amount of money you owe. High net worth is the benefit of investing in real estate long-term. It can support you financially in many ways and, in particular, with achieving and living your lifestyle goals. In our case, it helped finance international travel to support our first daughter to compete around the world on the Canadian National Rhythmic Gymnastics Team. We were able to fund our second daughter's equestrian life, including more than ten years of lessons and competitions, leading up to her competing at one of the top equestrian events in Canada, The Royal Winter Fair. We've also enjoyed traveling to more than 20 countries including France, Japan and Spain. All of this is a result of having built up good positive cash flow and equity in buying our neighbours' houses. Buying just one of your neighbours' houses will set you up nicely to support your retirement years.

WHY BUY YOUR NEIGHBOUR'S HOUSE?

There are the obvious financial and lifestyle advantages to buying real estate as discussed above, but why, specifically, am I recommending you that buy your neighbour's house? How often have you driven by a house in your own neighbourhood and wondered to yourself "how much does that house cost?" Have you thought fleetingly, "I wonder if we could purchase that house?" Some of the reasons for buying and owning one (or more) of your neighbours' houses include:

1. It is easy to maintain your neighbour's house and meet with its tenants.

It takes much less time to service your properties, meet with tenants and handle maintenance issues when they are right next door. One of the disadvantages of owning real estate in other cities is that tenants have a track record of not showing up when they say they will. If that happens and your house is next door, there's no travel time lost, and it's not a big deal. Meeting a plumber who is doing work on your property is also more convenient. The time savings of managing property close by are significant.

2. You'll be motivated to keep them in good condition.

You won't forget to cut the grass or take care of maintenance issues as you will take pride in having the houses that are next to you look good. Unfortunately, that is not the case with some landlord owned properties in remote cities. You can often spot the landlord owned properties as the ones with uncut grass and houses with maintenance issues. When properties are well maintained and cared for, they'll be worth more money and rent for a higher dollar amount.

3. You have a natural screen against attracting "bad" tenants.

Selecting good tenants is important to your success as a landlord. Any "bad" tenant who is likely to cause you issues or not pay rent will likely not apply to live in your house, choosing instead to live somewhere else. It's too easy for a landlord who lives next door to know when the tenant is home and follow up directly for any payment or concerns, for example, partying or loud music. But if a "good" tenant likes you and the property, they'll see it as an advantage that their landlord lives close by, so that they can look after maintenance issues quicker. We have had a 15-year excellent track record of attracting good tenants in our "neighbour" houses.

4. Improvements to your house will add value to your house "next door."

Curb appeal matters and being able to control and enhance the streetscape of multiple properties side by side will increase their overall value. Curb appeal is the first impression someone has of your house, either positive or negative. When you own two, three or more homes on your own street, making "curb appeal" improvements is a benefit to all of them, in addition to making you feel good about how they look. Spending $5,000 in improvements on one of the houses could multiply the overall value to your streetscape by a two to three times multiplying factor.

Landscaping is a good example of an exterior improvement that improves curb appeal. This helps when you go to the bank for financing, and they send out a bank appraiser to appraise the value of your house(s), as the properties will appraise at a higher value. If you ever decide to sell one of your houses, the ability to ensure that they all are in top shape and look good from the street is in your total control. That is not always the case. Some people find when they go to sell a home, the house next door detracts from the streetscape and value of their home. Some of the things we've done to our homes over the years include:

- Upgraded our driveways from gravel to pavement with perimeter pavers
- Added interlocking pathways to the doorsteps
- Hired a landscape architect to design a circular garden with perennials and a landscape planter
- Installed heritage house number signs
- Contracted front porch restorations to remedy the impacts of age and weather
- Hired an architect and professional carpenter to design and build two heritage swing entry gates leading from the front to the rear of each property
- Updated porch / exterior lighting fixtures

With these types of exterior improvements to your homes, you will improve the overall value of your homes dramatically and feel good about doing so. Nobody will call you a "slumlord" when you own beautifully cared for homes with curb appeal.

5. They're easier to rent for a higher price as a "furnished rental."

Most home rentals are rented as unfurnished houses on a one-year lease. With your house being just next door, operating your homes as furnished rentals can be done by yourself easily, improving your positive cash flow. Think Airbnb, Vacation Rentals by Owner (VRBO) or short-term rentals on KIJIJI. As a furnished rental, tenants will pay a higher premium for rent as you will be providing the house with furniture, bedding and other accessories.

This provides a financial "up-side" to your rental revenue which could boost your positive cash flow by more than 50%. This could also make the difference as to whether or not your property will produce a positive cash flow. With a furnished rental, you'll be allowing tenants to move in with just a suitcase as if they were checking into a hotel. The types of people looking for furnished rentals include:

- Corporate executives or professionals
- Homeowners during major renovations
- Homeowners dealing with insurance claim disasters (i.e. house fire, flooding)
- Marital breakups. This is a big source for our tenants, who often need a place for an "open-ended" period of time while they figure out next steps, often up to one year, or more.
- People and families in transition. Often a couple or family will want to live in an area for a while before they decide if the area is the place they want to establish roots and purchase a house.

Our experience is that you can furnish an entire house for less than $10,000 and achieve payback within 18 months. The type of furnishings and services you'll need to provide will include kitchen utensils and accessories, beds and bedding, towels and linens, furniture, HDTV, artwork / décor, wireless internet, heat and hydro. You can hire a cleaner to perform a professional and thorough clean between tenants, or you can do this yourself.

6. You'll always know how your investment is performing.

You have a full view of your investment and can keep an eye on each house just by looking down (or up) the street. When you own traditional investments like stocks or mutual funds, you may not look at their performance or follow them closely enough to know how they are doing. You also have no control over how the company is managed or is performing. When you own property on the same street, you can't help but know how your houses are doing. If there's a problem with the roof and you notice shingles on the driveway after a windstorm, you can act on it right away before the roof leaks.

7. You can paint the houses your own colour scheme, increasing their market value.

You have total control over any paintable surfaces on your houses such as siding and door colours. Have someone you know or hire someone who is good with colours to help pick your colour scheme. This too helps with improving the "curb appeal." We painted all four of our houses a colour scheme based on an affirmation I learned while attending a seminar hosted by my karate sensei in the late 1980's. The affirmation "I am Happy, Healthy, Wealthy and Wise" has been a central and major influence in my life. I felt so strongly about this affirmation that more than 20 years ago I developed a system for filing my goals into these categories and gave each category a colour: the colour Blue for "Happy"—Blue Sky, Blue Water, Calmness; The colour Red for Healthy"—Red Blood, Red Tomatoes, Red Apples; The colour Green for "Wealthy"—Money and Wealth; and the colour Grey for "Wise"—Wise elders (and their grey hair). My wife and I chose to have our four Gables On The Park homes painted these four colours as part of our streetscaping and restoration improvement plan. For before and after photos, visit www.GablesOnThePark.com. The reason these unique colour choices work is that our homes are Victorian-era homes with intricate gingerbread and gables, which are known to be painted special colours during a restoration process. We were inspired by the famous San Francisco "Painted Ladies" homes, which are some of the most photographed houses in the world. But the bottom line is that when you own your own street someday, you too can choose your own colour scheme and improve their curb appeal. Please take a photo and send me the before and after photos!

HOW TO BUY YOUR NEIGHBOUR'S HOUSE.

The steps to follow in buying your neighbours house are:

1. Determine if buying your neighbour's house makes financial sense.

Since your neighbour's house is likely to be similar to your house, you can roughly figure out the carrying costs by basing the calculation on your current expenses and adjusting for the current market. Based on the estimated market value of the house, you can figure out what it would cost for another mortgage. Add to that the costs for property taxes and any other carrying costs, noting that in most rentals the tenants will pay the utility costs, including heat and hydro. Then research or ask around for what tenants in your area are paying per month to rent a house. Get some help online or from a realtor friend if you are not sure how to make this calculation. If the rent you can charge is higher than the expenses you will pay, the decision to buy your neighbour's house makes financial sense.

If the numbers don't add up keep in mind that it may be possible or necessary to renovate your neighbour's house to maximize your monthly income by adding a second suite such as a basement apartment. Sometimes this is required to make the property "cash flow" and is worth the time and effort to do so. Also consider the furnished rental option described above, which is another method to increase the rent amount.

2. Approach your neighbours to let them know you might be interested

if they were ever to sell.

Casually find out which of your neighbours are likely to be moving on within the next few years. For some, it could be highly unlikely, and for others, it could be sooner than you think. Depending on your relationship with your neighbours, you could even mention that you've read this book and are just curious about your long-term options. The other strategy is to just wait for a house on your street to get listed by a realtor. At that point, you can decide to pursue this strategy aggressively.

3. **Get pre-qualified by your bank.**

A key concept is that once you have developed equity in your primary residence, your bank will allow you to borrow against that equity to fund the down payment of your first investment property. It is possible that you can finance your entire down payment without coming up with additional money from other sources, based on the equity you hold in your primary residence. Approach your bank and ask them the question. They can do a rough calculation for you based on the approximate market value of your current house.

4. **Choose a realtor to help you transact the purchase.**

Since purchasing a house is such an important and significant financial transaction, you should seek the services of a qualified realtor to help you with the transaction. In our case, we purchased two of our three neighbours' homes without using a realtor, and one using the seller's realtor. But if we were to do this again, I would seriously consider hiring a realtor representing us as the buyer. We missed doing a home inspection on the purchase of one of our homes that a realtor would have recommended we do. A realtor will also take the pressure off of negotiating the best purchase price possible and completing all the paperwork correctly.

5. **Be ready to buy when the opportunity presents itself.**

With this real estate strategy, the key is to understand that when the opportunity presents itself, you have to be ready to act. Discuss with your partner and create a general agreement that you want to follow this strategy. When the third house on our street came up for sale, we had no forewarning, and we purchased the house the very night the for-sale sign went up. You may need to have patience as this strategy may take years to unfold, as it did in our case.

BUT WHAT IF YOU HAVEN'T PURCHASED YOUR FIRST HOUSE YET?

Don't worry if you have yet to purchase your first house as your primary residence. You have the added benefit of finding a neighbourhood where, once the time is right, this strategy could work. Look for neighbourhoods with homes that would provide you with a positive cash flow (the rental income will exceed the cost of your expenses, e.g. (mortgage, taxes etc.). Generally, this applies to starter homes. Buy in an up and coming location. Your investment will be improved dramatically if you can find a good location that is on its way up in value due to good demographics (people statistics), such as the number of people moving into your neighbourhood, their average income levels, etc. These are influenced by things that are happening in your neighbourhood to make it a more desirable place to live, such as improvements to the transportation system, urbanization and close proximity to water or a natural feature.

The strategy of buying your neighbour's house won't work in all situations. It won't work in high priced neighbourhoods where it's impossible to produce a positive cash flow (when your rental income is less than what you spend to own the property). It also won't work in locations where it's hard to rent. But don't worry. Most people have access to great investment properties within a one-to-two-hour radius of where they live. The key is to buy investment real estate, but start by looking on your own street and then in your own neighbourhood.

THE BIG PAYOFF

After paying off the mortgage for 25 years (the typical mortgage period on a house), you'll retire your debt with the bank and own the house outright. This will help you tremendously in your retirement years as now the money you were paying to the bank for your mortgage will become extra positive cash flow that will help you out in retirement years. Because your house was purchased next door or on your street, you'll have no problems continuing to rent out the house with minimal effort, as you've been doing for the past 25 years. It's like you developed a "money tree" in your own neighbourhood which keeps on giving. The house will also be worth hundreds of thousands of dollars. You could also consider selling and living off the proceeds from the sale of your house(s). You could downsize and live elsewhere, perhaps in a smaller and more affordable house in order to live off of all the equity you accumulated over the years of being a real estate investor on your own street.

It's also possible that you'll be approached by a developer to sell your homes if you happen to have purchased the house(s) next door. If you own land in a municipality where your zoning permits higher density housing, this could turn out to be a highly profitable strategy. And if you are entrepreneurial and want to be your own developer, you could develop the site yourself. It could be worth the time, effort and risk if you are up for it. In our own city, there are numerous sites where developers have been purchasing adjacent homes and businesses with the goal of getting approval to tear them down and build something grander.

The equity you gain from owning real estate will give you a huge advantage to help you do other amazing things. This principle alone has supported our family well over the past 25 years and allowed us to purchase our additional properties which led to us owning our street. It has also given us the financial resources to support our children with their extracurriculars, and family travel, as our net worth has grown.

WHAT DOES IT TAKE TO DO THIS?

Developing wealth as an active real estate investor does require you to have good ambition. It involves a willingness to take on some risk. It helps if you can develop some handyman skills or find someone you trust to do that for you. It takes an attitude to treats tenants like you'd like to be treated yourself. When issues come up dealing with tenants or maintenance, you'll need to focus on why you're doing this and the long-term benefits.

Owning physical real estate isn't for everyone. You need to have a certain temperament to deal with the tenants and maintenance issues or trust others to look after these things for you. For those who can never see themselves as landlords, there are other ways to benefit in real estate. For example, as a silent partner in a joint venture agreement or investor in a real estate investment trust (REIT). REIT's were established for small investors who were not interested in the responsibilities of property maintenance or managing tenants directly. REIT's are intended for people who want to be able to invest in real estate without the large capital required to purchase real estate directly.

Being goal driven was one of the reasons that led my wife Kathy and I to be successful not only with real estate but in other areas of life. In my book, 100 Life Goals, I write about 100 goals that will transform your life and give you the confidence to make the kind of decisions that will lead to success in real estate and other areas.

WHAT NEXT?

After following the advice on the "how to" section above, you could join a local real estate club to see other real estate investors in action and learn from them. I'm fortunate to be a member of a local real estate investment club, Rock Star Real Estate, that is helping hundreds of real estate investors achieve financial independence, with their slogan "Your Life, Your Terms." Once they heard of our story and strategy, they asked me to present to their members at one of their events on "Owning an Entire Street: How to go from one property to Owning the Whole Street." They also helped our daughter purchase her first investment property, a century duplex townhouse.

While it's rather intuitive that owning properties close to home makes the most sense, owning investment properties on the same street is not something that happens too often and is likely not something that would be discussed at a local real estate club. My hope is that in reading about this strategy, you develop the awareness that if one of your neighbours' houses comes up for sale, you take a serious look at whether this strategy could work for you. If you do, I'd love to hear about your story someday. Contact me through www.100GoalsClub.com.

Twice The Retirement For Half The Effort

A Baby Boomer's Guide to Profitable Apartment Investing

DR. JAMES MCQUISTON

Let's face it. There are many so-called experts in property investing, and there is no dearth of information on how to make it rich...quick. When push comes to shove, very few retirees make it beyond the first property investment, let alone to the top of the property ladder.

Why you may ask? You're smart and savvy, you've made it so far and are sitting on top of a very nice nest-egg. You most certainly won't make the same mistakes that have dogged those less lucky. However, from our viewpoint as property investors, the field or property investing is riddled with potholes for beginners.

Here are some of the common pitfalls: making a decision based on emotions rather than hard, cold facts, rushing in without doing sufficient homework just because someone else appeared interested in the same property. On the other hand, you could be procrastinating so much that the property is snapped up by other more astute investors. And the most common blight of all on beginning investors?

Poor cash flow management. Not understanding the costs involved in buying and holding onto property. Not accounting for or failing to plan and set aside funds for unexpected contingencies. Such contingencies include unplanned maintenance repairs, extended vacancies, bad tenants, high turnover rates. Then again, there is choosing the wrong type of property, in the wrong neighborhood, at the wrong time of the investing cycle by buying high and selling low.

I'm not saying that property investing is not for baby boomers. On the contrary, investing in property, significantly in apartments, is a proven strategy to accumulate wealth and generate handsome double-digit returns. You have to do it right.

WILL YOUR MONEY LAST AS LONG AS YOU?

Now as a baby boomer, you've some very real concerns. If your money is relatively dormant, you may not be earning more than 4% and the most important question you have is:

How long will your money last?

The math is not in your favour. According to the Employment Benefits Research Institute (ebri.org), 43% of baby boomers are at risk of running out of money. Our figures show that by the age of 75, at least half the baby boomers will run out of money. How much you take out of your retirement savings each year will affect how long the money will last.

Of course, if you draw down by 4% every year, your retirement savings will last for 25 years. But will a 4% withdrawal rate be sufficient for the lifestyle you've grown accustomed to? The numbers tell all. If you've saved $250,000, withdrawing 4% a year means you have to live off $10,000 for 12 months. If you take out much more, your money will run out faster! The numbers tell all. (see Table 1)

Increasing your withdrawal rate to 6% means you will run dry in 16.6 years and to 8% implies that you will have no savings left in 12.5 years. Not an optimistic picture, is it?

In Table 1, which displays the relationship between annual withdrawal rates from savings and time left to the portfolio, we assume $250,000 in retirement savings and an annual appreciation in the portfolio equal to inflation.

Table 1: **Impact of Differing Withdrawal Rates on a $250,000 Retirement Portfolio**

Withdrawal Rate	Annual Withdrawals	Time in years before money runs out
4%	$10,000	25
6%	$15,000	16.6
8%	$20,000	12.5
10%	$25,000	10

LEVERAGING TO GET DOUBLE DIGIT RETURNS

In a Federal Reserve Survey of Consumer Finances completed in 2012, it showed that equities account for a substantial part of assets held by baby boomers. In fact, the Investment Company Institute in a recent Wall Street Journal reports that more than a quarter of investors have 100% of their IRA's invested in stocks – including those between 60 and 64 years old. Another 16% have 80% of their IRA's invested in the stock market. However, how much of a return have these investors derived from stocks?

Figures of indexed funds offered to the public sector through The Federal Thrift Savings Plans showed domestic stocks posted an average of 7.44% returns over the past 10 years. Small stocks did better with a 10.4% return but bonds and money markets only returned between 3.4%-4.6% to investors every year for 10 years.

The issue is if inflation is 3% a year, how safe are your 4% returns? Not very secure is the answer. With such concerns to address, how do you go about changing the math in your favor?

The answer lies in leveraged appreciation, which you create by implementing these four steps.

1. Buy undervalued properties with upside potential
2. Upgrade the properties and raise rents accordingly
3. Leverage the property through financing
4. Pay off the mortgage through rental payments from tenants

Apartment complexes are valued differently from residential properties. When you are shopping around for a house, the appraiser will value it according to the most recent transactions of houses of comparable sizes in your neighborhood. An apartment complex, on the other hand, is determined by the cash flow i.e. the rental income received less any outgoings for maintenance, debt service, management, and property taxes.

Therefore, if you can find an apartment complex, which is overdue for a remodel or facelift, in a nice neighborhood and which is struggling with a 70% occupancy rate, you are well-poised to earn double digit returns.

Let's walk through how it works in real life.

You find an apartment with deferred maintenance and high vacancy near 70%; since it is a little shabby and out of style, you are likely to buy it for at least a 20% discount. You put a down payment of 33 1/3 % of the negotiated price.

Next, you remodel the unoccupied units and when leases expire and the tenants move out, you upgrade those units and raise rents by 4% across the board. This process spreads out over four years to give time for existing leases to terminate, for phased remodeling and for the increased rents to take root, so to speak.

Here is how you gain leverage through borrowings. If you put a down payment of 33 1/3% and borrow the remaining 66 2/3%, you have established a 3:1 leverage. In other words, if the apartment complex was worth $1,000,000, you put down $333,000 but because you control the ownership of 100% of the building, you get all the benefits, such as higher rents that accrue to the entire upgraded building. (As an aside, making at least a 30% down payment opens up access to better financing terms and you won't have to pay such high interest rates on your borrowings)

Therefore, when you raise rents by 4% a year, you realize a gain of 4% on your down payment AND a gain 8% on your leveraged position, that is that portion of the investment financed with other people's money, greatly magnifying the returns on your apartment building.

Proceeding with this example, let's also say you amortize your debt over 25 years with 2% of the mortgage retired yearly

In summary, your annual rate of appreciation on your investment is made up of 4 components; remember we are assuming a 4-year holding period:

1. Purchase at 20% discount, amortized over 4 years. 5%
2. Increased rents after remodeling 4%
3. 8% on leveraged position (see above paragraphs) 8%
4. 2% of the borrowings paid off annually. 2%

Total annual appreciation 19%

The conclusion: In this example, using leverage significantly boosts your rate of return in apartment investing. By smart and strategic use of leverage in an appreciating asset, like apartment complexes, you are substantially increasing your net worth. Here is one more thought. In all likelihood, with the renovations enhancing the desirability of your building, you will attract more tenants and increase the occupancy rate from 70% to 90%. The higher occupancy rate translates to higher cash flow which, in turn boosts the value of the apartment complex by at least 20%.

The previous example is for demonstration purposes only and is no guarantee of future performance.

STRIKING IT HOT

Many investors have become wealthy through investing in apartments. However, those new to property investing in this sector hold the misperception that you require millions to make millions in apartment investing.

What if I told you that you can gain entry into this lucrative field and enjoy double-digit returns with as little as $25,000? Here is a chance to copy the moves of millionaires without having to start out with millions of your own money. Isn't that exciting and definitely worth exploring?

We titled this chapter ***Twice The Retirement for Half The Effort*** because we have proven it time and time again that investing in apartment complexes does work. Everyone needs a home and people don't move out just because the economy turns sour. If anything, a slower economy encourages downsizing from large houses with excess capacity to more affordable apartment living. With tenants on a lease, you receive a steady stream of cash flow; if you own a residential property as an investment, when the lease ends, you have no cash flow until you find a new tenant. Looking at your investment options in this light, apartment investing would appear to spread the risk over more rental units than putting your money into residential properties.

How would you then maximize your retirement savings to benefit from such kinds of leveraged appreciation?

First off, opt for a self-directed IRA. It gives you the option to safely control your own investments and to tax-defer any gains.

Next, you want to have your real estate team in place before you begin a search for property. You want to line up the financiers, the underwriters, the brokers, lawyers, property managers and contractors (for any renovations) because the real estate investor with the best professional resources will know which properties to ignore and which deserve careful consideration.

However, rather than assemble a group of professionals on your own steam, one plodding step at a time, we at United Equity Partners (UEP) offer you a ready-made team that has proven skills and a track record in successful investing. With our deep-domain expertise in real estate, we focus on underperforming niche markets with assets available for sale below market price.

You may have heard of Real Estate Investment Trusts (REITs) that promise a steady dividend payout. These large trusts focus on Grade A apartment buildings or other assets like office towers and shopping malls, which are already income producing and which require minimal maintenance and renovation. However, REITs pay a premium to invest in such quality buildings, which suggest that there is limited scope for asset appreciation.

HOW WE GET IT RIGHT AT TWICE THE RETIREMENT FOR HALF THE EFFORT

There is a common classification of property in commercial investing in which properties are categorized as A, B or C. At UEP, we have made a deliberate and strategic investment decision to focus on medium Class C and C+ apartments in B neighborhoods. Class C are properties which are older and which could significantly benefit from upgrades and renovations and even a change in management; B neighborhoods reflect a higher quality of consumers who will apply to live in the upgraded apartments.

Our strategy is to buy below market price and through careful upgrading and renovation, we add more value to the apartment complex than we have spent. The owners of these C or C+ properties are often either banks left holding foreclosures or distressed owners who are unable to service their debt or are tired of holding on to their underperforming assets. UEP takes them off their hands at a price that is fair to both parties.

We run through the figures carefully before inviting our future equity partners to join us. We handle our partner's money more conservatively than if it were our own before purchasing properties that UEP affiliates will manage. In our team of professionals are onsite managers who know how to add value through selected renovations, who know how much of a rent increase we can get after upgrades are completed and how to create incentives to attract a desirable class of tenants. Our underwriters perform the appropriate calculations to weigh risks against returns and will not make an offer on the property until we have conducted appropriate research and due diligence.

IS PROPERTY INVESTING RIGHT FOR ME?

If you are willing to hold an investment for the medium term to realize appreciable gains, you are right for apartment investing. Our holding period is 3-5 years. Of course, you may get faster returns in the stock market, but you have to make sure you buy early and sell at the right time before the markets top out. If you pull the trigger at the wrong time, it takes a considerable length of time to make good what you've lost. For example, to recover from a 20% loss, you need a 25% gain to break even. If you have suffered a drawdown on your capital of 25%, you need a 33% gain just to get back to your original capital. In order words, you need three right decisions to make up the losses from one wrong move.

Many retail investors in the stockmarket have been feeling that they have been served a raw deal. Not surprisingly. With technology like high frequency trading where sophisticated computerized programs make thousands of buy and sell decisions in less time than it took you to read half this sentence, and with billion dollar hedge funds influencing price and volumes, you are right to feel that way.

Bonds are predictable but after accounting for inflation, your bonds could be worth less at the end of the contract than when you first invested. In property investing, you need to be invested for a longer time, but if you choose correctly, your income stream is significantly less volatile and definitely more predictable since leases are typically signed for at least a year, if not more.

Further, at UEP, we tailor and align our investments to your objectives. We interview our investors to find out more about your investment expectations before inviting you to become equity partners in the appropriate portfolio of apartment investments.

All the professionals in our team are fully invested in making sure you are successful. Unlike in stockmarket funds where you have to pay a sales load to gain entry, we don't make money until you do. That differentiates us from other property investing funds. We work hard at seeking out investments that will produce a high enough profit margin so that everyone involved is profitably compensated.

WHY SHOULD I WORK WITH A TEAM?

We have an extensive network among banks, brokers, financiers, lawyers and contractors that an individual investor will find difficult to approximate. Remember the investor with the right combination of resources is able to move quickly when the right opportunities spring up. Being able to close a transaction fast enough is a significant advantage in any market, especially in properties.

We have established relationships with banks that have an inventory of homes and apartments, so we have access to good deals well before the individual investor gets wind of these opportunities. Brokers are willing to give us first look at new properties because they know that UEP has both the financial capacity and the willingness to close on desirable transactions. Finally, we are able to call on contractors who give us priority in remodeling because we provide them with consistent work.

If you were to undertake renovations on your own, how would you be able to gauge that the contractor is bidding accurately and is not going to surprise you, unpleasantly, with cost overruns when the final bill is to be paid?

That's what we mean that with UEP, you get ***Twice the Retirement for Half the Effort***. We put in all the hard work so you don't have to.

Here is an analogy I would like to share. When your car runs into problems, your first thought is to get it to the mechanic, isn't it? You don't instead think about buying a repair manual, get tools and diagnostic equipment, find a garage with a lift and get your hands all greasy and dirty. Unless you have the training and mindset of a car mechanic, you are likely not to be able to diagnose, troubleshoot and repair your car, not even if you are armed to the hilt with D-I-Y tutorials. Of course, you won't waste your time attempting to be your own car repairman because the mechanic is worth every dollar that you pay. You know without a doubt that he will be able to diagnose the problem and get it fixed, freeing you to focus on the important things that matter.

With that being said, why not go to the experts when it comes to investing in apartments? You reap the benefits of collective experience and significant economies of scale and every dollar you invest comes back to you multiplied.

Find out more about how to build your retirement wealth faster than you would be able to achieve on your own by visiting us at http://unitedequitypartners.com/. We have a wealth of free bonuses and tips on ways for you to make money in apartment investing. Take advantage of these ideas to accumulate wealth that you may be able to retire comfortably and confidently, secure in the knowledge that money will be there when you need it. It is time to take action to build your wealth responsibly, so act now, visit our website or email me at Mcquiston1999@gmail.com.

Dr. James McQuiston is a Senior Managing Partner of United Equity Partners, who identifies and selects real estate and business opportunities for the firm. Although he started out as an optometrist, he showed great skill and enjoyed significant success in commercial real estate investing and from that foundation, expanded his investments into residential and commercial properties in Texas, Oklahoma and Illinois. He has also co-founded an association of stock investors and managed several portfolios of blue-chip stocks. He donates his optometric skills to the underprivileged around the world and has been actively involved with Eye Projects on four continents.

Honor Your Inner Treasures

CELINA TIO

COLLECTIVE CREATED ME

"We are all created from our experiences, and the first step towards embracing our inner treasures is to acknowledge this. You are wonderful, and the experiences that took you to this point are all part of that. Do not be afraid of yourself; instead, let yourself shine." This quote is from my recent book, *Honor Your Inner Treasures*. It's an underlying principle of that work, and its message is most certainly applicable to what you're about to read in this chapter of *The Authorities*. Collective Created Me explains in the *Honor Your Inner Treasures* book, how most of our beliefs are obtained through training and repetition, and assumed personality through education. Becoming aware of the Collective Created Me is extremely beneficial because it puts you on the road to self-acceptance and realization, forgiveness, independence, appreciation and true happiness.

Think about this for a moment: do you remember someone in your family being sick when you were a child? Were the hours spent in family time talking about symptoms, where pain started, where it ended, how long it lasted, and medicines? It's likely that much of the conversation also revolved around nurses, doctors' assessments and trips to the hospital. Soon, with so much health and sickness related information taken in, you unconsciously started to become so familiar enough with that illness that you accepted it as just part of your family. It became so normal that you could quickly respond to questions about it as if it were your illness, too. "My uncle Charlie had it, and so did his son and my grandmother. It runs in our family."

Imagine if the conversation you heard about Uncle Charlie's illness had been about the way that healthy habits, physical activities, and letting go of toxic thoughts helped him recover. What would you have learned to do then in the event of an illness?

This example of negativity changing your perspective is applicable to other life experiences. What about love and relationships? Conversations about unfaithfulness, divorce, unhealthy relationships, abuse, violence? How has the negativity of those conversations affected your beliefs and the actions you've taken in life? Money is another example. People often say they never have enough money. Stories are shared about someone's new business failing, or friends who've lost their homes because they couldn't make their mortgage payments. Wouldn't stories of success have a more positive impact to encourage others to improve in their lives?

Most people receive diagnoses during their lives pertaining to health, personal finances, the country's economy, beauty, fashion and relationships. Usually, these diagnoses are fully accepted as truth and fact. There is an alternative, however. Why not see a diagnosis as feedback of that exact, precise moment and utilize it as the moment of opportunity to change, to create, to expand, to become, to discover, is opening up for you?

People often say when a door closes a window opens, and wait for the window to open right in front of them. Often, hoping that the window will magically pop open and the situation will change. The sad thing is, it may take a while and in the meantime the beliefs that life is not fair, life is hard or life is good to others start to run your thoughts.

I want you to know that all windows and doors are always open for you. Even more, there are no windows, there are no doors, because once you embrace your greatness you are free to live with purpose.

Going back to our example of listening to other people's life experiences, can you perceive how your fears and beliefs originated during these events? The occasions are wonderful moments to enjoy and remember the past, but sometimes people retell stories about illnesses with as much detail as they can recall. It's possible the now-adult children have no recollection of the event's seriousness because they remember with a child's naïveté only how happy they were about recovery. Now, listening to the story of an experience in your life that evoked sadness, these adults inevitably feel pulled down and relive that low-energy feeling. You can change that feeling in you and all the people around you. Next time you are at a reunion be sure to evoke moments that bring joy and laughter. Everyone will leave feeling great, having enjoyed the party, and with a more positive attitude for the next adventure in their life.

BECOME AWARE - CONNECT WITH YOUR INNER BEING

Let go of the stories and let go of others' experiences. Start living your own.

Embrace the belief that your life is complete and absolute just as is. Take a deep breath, aware of your body, starting at the top and working your way down. Begin with your scalp, your hair, your temples, your forehead, your eyebrows, your eyes, then move on until you reach the tip of your toes. It's important to take in every part of yourself so don't stop at the surface. Recognize your organs and their functions, even noting your breath as it travels into your lungs and fills you with pure oxygen. Become aware of your being. I ask that you become aware of your being, not that you look into the mirror or take a selfie and analyze it to see if you have wrinkles, or criticize your body shape. Stop judging yourself and start knowing yourself.

Selfies have become, to many, a tool to prove oneself, or a tool of confirmation of existence, presence and self-acceptance, and others' approval of the moment that is being lived.

As if the moment being lived needs external approval to be considered as a "perfect moment" and only then sharing it with the world.

When you look at the moment you are living as an image that "looks good" or "like happiness", the gap between what you are doing "looks great", and truly feeling great, is large. There is no enjoyment or happiness if it always depends on others' opinions. Making a picture look good when the emotions you are feeling at the moment don't match the illusion of the created image is keeping you from living a true honest happy moment.

Different from this is taking a picture to capture a moment of real pleasure and happiness, and the peace and joy that healthy relationships and celebrations bring. Those are photographs that recall true emotions of happiness, in turn aligning your whole being into feeling truly amazing. These selfies are not only a moment taken with a camera; they are taken into your soul, leaving a long-lasting impression in your life. Those are moments that you will truly love to share with others without deleting anything. What is your selfie telling you when you look at it? What is that image revealing?

Become aware of yourself and the moment without editing. Be completely honest about everything. In this moment of self-awareness, accept everything – your age, aches, sadness, longings, best memories, dreams – without shyness, even if they look too big at this moment. Become aware because for the first time in your life you will be truly, honestly and entirely present with yourself, as you know yourself to be at this moment. What is your inner self telling you? This is the true SELF you should be contemplating.

If you do this, for the first time in your life you will be truly, honestly and entirely present. Your unique, true self will be revealed. For many people, doing this will be the scariest meeting of their lives. To me it is the most amazing!

When working with my clients, this point of their journey is the most exciting to me. As their guide to reaching their true inner being throughout the Honor Your Inner Treasures™ Program, the transformation the client undergoes is magical, because their life suddenly expands as they embrace and accept fully their inner self.

YOUR EMOTIONS ARE POWERFUL. LEARN FROM THEM.

Pretending is the only sure thing someone does when they are denied their true feelings. Pretending to feel well, smiling just with the movement of the facial muscles, repeating clichés as a consolation to true feelings, and distancing ourselves from loved ones or hiding from life aren't effective measures. Not talking about problems doesn't solve them. On the contrary, the repetition of those actions and inner messages undoubtedly becomes the reality in your life, which extends the sadness, insecurity, lack of confidence, and low-energy life. It's an unhealthy cycle, difficult to break. Have you ever heard people complaining about the good luck of others, or blaming the sad circumstances in their life on other people's lives? If you come close to a person behaving this way, stay away. You don't want to adopt that attitude.

You can change, you can become more, and you can be the best amazing you because you truly, genuinely feel it. Sharing your life with others with honesty, because there is absolutely nothing to hide, is liberating. Accept that you are a human being experiencing life, and in the process are growing, becoming, expanding, and evolving.

Through this process there will be moments that call for change, whether of habits, beliefs, actions, or behaviors. Change is a process of evolving into a different state. The emotions that you carry through the transition are of most importance. Are you making the change out of resentment or fear? Is it happening because you don't feel you're enough? Or are you just resigning yourself because you are obedient to unhappiness. What if you make the change because you know that you would love and enjoy doing something different?

Ask yourself what you need to make this change? Maybe it's taking a course or learning something new. Going through training is a fun ride when all you are doing is acquiring new skills to master what you love to do! Don't let the fear of change keep you from becoming healthier and happier. You look and feel healthy and beautiful when you are enjoying the moments that you are creating in your life. Change gives you jolts of energy that propels you to do more.

CHANGE TO THE POSITIVE SIDE OF LIFE

"Change the thinking positive and acting negative attitude." – Celina Tio

I hear people talking about difficult situations in their lives that end with usual comments like "I'm staying positive," "I'm trying to think positive" or "Hopefully…" However, simply repeating the mantra "I'm staying positive" does not make it true. When you are vibrating in the true sense of positive energy your life has no room for negative energy. Positive will always see, hear, understand, interpret, and plan in a constructive manner. When clients come for their first consultations with me, I listen attentively to their voices. From their tones I can hear the negative energy of unhealed wounds, regardless of the words they use. They tell their stories as if they've become comfortable hurting. This is a common means of self-defense and emotional survival.

In their journeys through the Honor Your Inner Treasures™ Program, clients delve into their true selves and are guided through the process of transmuting their thoughts into a positive perspective. This transformation occurs once we do the necessary inner work at the soul level, which is the purest essence of being. Anger may become understanding and compassion; resentment an opportunity for self-reflection and inner growth; and solitude a time of self-forgiveness and self-acceptance. The more you discover about your inner being, the closer you are to the positive energy of your true self. Knowing that each step my clients take brings them closer to their inner being of positive creation gives me great joy. It is important to create life experiences in such a way that, when you reflect on the past, all you see is a magical garden of your own design that you can be proud of having imagined, lived, grown and created.

Let's do an exercise that will assist you with looking at decisions based on fear. You will need to sit comfortably on a chair and have with you a pad of paper and a pen. Imagine an "X" mark on the floor to your right that represents the change that you want to make, and an "X" to your left side. The "X" mark on the left side represents the negative reasons that you have to make the change in your life and the "X" on the right side represents positive ones.

On the paper write the reasons you want to make the change. For example, let's say that the decision you want to make is about a change in career. Write on the paper the thoughts that have crossed your mind. Use one piece of paper per thought about the issue. (It is important to follow these steps carefully.) Now, decide if the thought you've written is negative or positive and put the paper to your left or right side. Use the guide on page 9 to help you determine whether your thoughts are positive or negative.

As you can see, on the column for thoughts I have underlined the negative comments. On the fourth example the word but is underlined because the "buts" are so big in our lives. You truly have to listen closely when you speak. Until you change your internal dialogue and are able to do this spontaneously, it is best to do this exercise by writing it on pieces of paper. Doing this will change the thinking positive and acting negative attitude that most people have without realizing why their lives are so difficult. Once you have identified your thought process about the issue, you can transform it and move all your thoughts to the positive side.

When you finish transforming your thought process, written now with only positive reasons, you will feel much more enthusiastic and energized to move forward and take the necessary steps to become or do. Every step of the way becomes more pleasurable because you have created a happy and positive future for yourself. What seemed to be big obstacles in the road are now the building stones and success is within reach! Congratulations! You truly do have the inner power to transform your life.

I have created a transformational workbook for my clients that enter the Honor Your Inner Treasures™ Program and as we go through the process they do simple, fun and motivating change processes. When they finish, only then the realization comes regarding how powerful it is to invest time into loving ourselves.

BELIEFS

All people have beliefs that help structure their lives. We know with great certainty that whatever we believe is true, and one of these beliefs is self-worth. People even determine their income based on their belief of self-worth. Your resume indicates exactly how much money you will make in the next year. When you review it and no changes have been made, you are hoping that inflation or the economy of the company you work for will determine the increase in the salary that you will be earning. Have you ever stopped to think about it? You are giving your power to another person to determine your growth, not only in your economy, but also your personal potential to do more, to become who you want to be.

I have worked with clients who are business owners feeling stressed out because of low funds, poor self-esteem and a lack of confidence. These issues not only impact their personal lives but also how their business grows. Those negative beliefs, ideas and limitations also have an impact on their earnings and the status of their finances, and all the people working for their company.

I remember working with Priti, a 43-year-old married woman. She emigrated to Canada from India, where she had received her degree as a software engineer. Once in Canada, Priti was able to obtain a position where she could use some of her education and experience. The reason I say 'some' of her education and experience is because when she came to see me for the first time she said that she was starting to feel bored with her job and not living up to her full potential. Priti felt that there were problems in the company that took too long to solve and required great work to make operations run more efficiently. Doing things the way the company had done for years was causing the same problems over and over again. She wanted to make a change and had a vision to do so.

However, Priti was quiet and didn't like to be the center of attention, so she kept to herself, trying to fit into the company's mold. Eventually, the conflict between shyness and wanting to change operations caused her a great deal of stress. She could not feel confident putting forth her suggestions. And although there was nothing I could do to help her with her software issues, I was able to help her build her confidence to act, speak, think and move forward. With those new positive traits, she was able to increase her self-esteem and recognize her own value.

Being foreign and fearing she might appear ignorant to others was one of Priti's greatest stumbling blocks. To offset this, I offered a metaphor. I asked her to consider the plastic casing that envelops the computer containing the software she created. Is that foreign? Obviously, the answer is no. The casing is just another part of the whole computer just as she, too, is part of the whole.

In creation nothing is foreign. We are all co-creating contributing our energy into the amazing universe we all live in. This is why it is so important that you truly live your lives from your inner treasures because underneath your fears and doubts you are pure potential, everyone has amazing positive energy to add to the whole.

We also worked on Priti's self-esteem and confidence by training her subconscious mind to act, feel and think the way the leader she desired to be would. The leader she wanted to be was one who confidently and clearly communicated her views, ideas and solutions with the tone of a manager. In just a few weeks Priti noticed she was expressing her ideas, asking questions and sharing her knowledge and experience without feeling timid. Most importantly, she noticed that her peers welcomed her ideas.

Eventually, Priti realized this company didn't have potential to grow and she was putting all of her potential in a box too small for her. She knew she was ready to move on with confidence.

That spark of inner realization of your personal self, and of how truly valuable your contribution is to everything you do, changes everything. You become confident to plan and live your life making decisions that feel right, and feel an inner peace because you gained control. Now, you have the power to do the things that are truly important to you. Once you learn to expand your consciousness beyond your fear, the limitation you had becomes limit-less.

In my upcoming book, *Limitless Beliefs - 7 Steps to Transcend into a Joyful and Abundant You*, you will find the how-to for this process. To purchase, learn more about the book, www.limitlessbeliefs.com or www.celinatioauthor.com.

YOUR LIFE IS YOUR DECISION AND YOUR CREATION

"Create your life experiences in such a way that the day you look back all you see is a magical garden of your own design that you can be proud of having imagined,

lived, grown and created." – *Celina Tio*

"Really? Are you sure? Because I was told…" These are all comments based on a lack of confidence. This does not have to be you! You are able to declare your independence, power and freedom! To embrace the true and pure intention of creation!

I'll share with you the experience of Laura, a beautiful and intelligent woman who came to my office for help. As she introduced herself and explained the reason why she had made the appointment, I was amazed. At 32 years old, she was a successful fashion designer. Her passion, however, was singing and songwriting. What an amazing girl, and what a disparity in her professional career compared to her dreams.

Her narrative was sad due to many of her life's circumstances and events. Her self-esteem and confidence was at an all-time low after ending a relationship that was going nowhere. Now, she hoped to let go of all her little self. Laura wanted to have more confidence to make decisions and communicate her ideas and feelings, and she wanted to feel good about herself. Simply put, she wanted to live happily.

I could have told her how beautiful, amazing and intelligent I thought she was. I could have pointed out all the wonderful opportunities she could have in life or how much I admired her. But she wasn't there for me to tell her what most any friend would. She needed to know from her own heart, discovering and loving herself so that she could go through her life's journey knowing her essence.

At the end of her journey I asked Laura to write what she decided was most valuable about herself. She took a few days and sent me an e-mail describing her value as she perceived it. Imagine the courage it took to be so vulnerable. Without relying on anyone else's opinions, she confessed her own beauty, strength, warmth and intelligence. She had honored her inner treasures.

I have asked her permission to share this with you because I want you to know that it is also possible for you. She kindly and happily agreed because she felt she could help other people. Maybe that person today is you or someone you love.

"I value myself because I am a strong person who perseveres through hardship, and I have faith I will get through it. I value myself because I am loving and kind-hearted person. I value myself because I take care of those in need and treat them just as I would treat myself. I value myself because I am a hard worker and very motivated. I value myself because I am a good woman. I value myself because I have self-respect and integrity, and will not allow anyone to take that away. I value myself because I am humble in life. I value myself because I am a good sister, friend, daughter, and lover because I care for people's feelings. I value myself because of my relationship with God and how I want to continue to help myself be better. I value myself because I am a loving woman who shares love with everyone. I value myself because I can make people laugh and really bring out the best in them; this shows me how amazing I am. I value myself because even if I am scared or fearful I have courage to face those fears. I value myself because of my ability to forgive and make amends even when people have truly hurt me. I value my positive thinking and my ability to turn what can be a bad situation into a great one. I value myself because I am able to express my feelings and my emotions now in a calm and mature way. I value myself because any goal I set for myself I achieve, because I am willing to work hard. I value myself because I always keep on smiling even when the going gets tough. I value myself because I am beautiful, strong, smart, mature, funny, loving, and kind person."

- Laura, Toronto, Canada
Fashion Designer/ Singer and Songwriter, naturally from the heart.

APPRECIATION

If life were a coin, would you say it is less valuable when you are looking on the head side just because the imprinted value is on the other side and you can't see it?

The value of everything is found through deep appreciation. Lots of people walk through life with the expectation of being accepted and liked by others, but they suffer a great deal when the world around them doesn't show them what they expect. Start increasing your self-value by appreciating your life as it is in this moment. Even if your world looks or feels different than you'd like, there is value to be found. You can increase that value by describing it and saying thank you. At first, it might take some creativity if you have been depreciating things most of your life.

Let's think of something you do every day, like eating. All of us eat when we are hungry, but some also eat when anxious, nervous or depressed. There is even a name for this: comfort food. Comfort food is supposed to make you feel better when you eat it; however, nobody has ever said, "I was feeling sad and I ate a whole bowl of ice cream and now everything is fine! All of a sudden I feel loved and my finances have improved drastically with every spoonful of food I ate!" This would simply not be true.

On the other hand, when you eat because you feel hungry your body and mind feel better because they receive the nourishment needed. If you offer and share your meal and spend time in the company of family or friends, your soul is nourished as well. In preparing your meal, be grateful that you have the ingredients on hand needed to prepare the meal that will nourish every cell in your body. Imagine all the minerals, vitamins, proteins, carbohydrates and fibers that are present in what you are about to consume, and how you are benefiting from them. Thank the supermarket for having them available for you, and the people who've dedicated their life into growing them. Even thank the work you do that earns you the funds to buy your food. It's crucial to become aware of the dimension of what you are about to eat.

- Be grateful to the soil that has the perfect nutrients to grow your food.
- Be grateful to the sun and the water for adding their energy.
- Be grateful to the universe for having created a planet that contains everything you need.
- Be grateful for the beauty of the colors, textures and aromas of the vegetables, herbs or fruits, or a cup of coffee.
- Be grateful to the person who will share this meal with you.
- Be grateful that you can share your moment with that person and have each other's company.
- Be grateful that you have the ability to offer and share your meal.
- Be grateful that life is allowing this moment to sit, rest, replenish, keep each other's company and share whatever it is that needs to be shared at the moment.

By now, appreciation has started to flow from the heart and you will know if what you are about to eat is healthy for you. If you have to thank the chemicals named on the package that are so difficult to pronounce instead of the natural sweet aroma of a natural ripe tomato, you will know not to eat it. Your body will show you resistance. When appreciation flows from the heart, you will feel true comfort even when you drink plain water. Do it at your next meal. Do the same with your home, your family, your pet and your neighbor.

Practicing heartfelt appreciation will change your perspective on life.

SELF-REALIZATION

"You have the power of pure energy within you to be, to do, to have, to accomplish, to become your dream." – Celina Tio

When you truly know your essence, everything changes easily. Your relationships are healthier by helping you grow with people who share your life's path. Life becomes pleasurable and enjoyable, and conflict and stress no longer emanate from you. You understand that ego makes peoples lives sad and full of problems, and that it drives competition, fear, war and destruction.

Knowing your essence also means the things that you're doing now are in line with what makes you feel happy. It's easy to identify if you're off balance because life no longer feels whole. You become aware of your energy and how it affects everything around you. You have a fresh understanding that you are part of creation, co-creating with all that makes us one.

You become more independent when you know your essence, investing into your wellbeing and happiness instead of things that have no value to your personal self. Rich and wealthy has a whole different meaning now. No more spending to do things or obtain things just because you feel bored or empty. You'll no longer feel the need to shop in an attempt to feel happy or, even worse, to look happy. You become independent and know that you are the only one responsible for how you are living your life, with no one else to blame. Vacationing to escape from reality is a thing of the past. Instead, you'll have the freedom to choose a destination that will give you enjoyment in everything from the planning to the adventure to the return.

At this point, inner peace has become real in your life and you'll have the self-realization that you truly are the creator of every moment in your life. Your future is right this moment, so make it amazing and wonderful. Move from the comfort spot of sameness, obedience and unhappiness. Walking on your self-pity will take you only to more of the same. It is time to tell yourself that you deserve to experience life, and to savor and indulge in the sweetness and pure love of creation. You deserve to feel free of unnecessary pain, have inner peace and feel truly loved.

Of course we all have sad moments in our lives. It is normal to experience loss and birth, laughter with tears of joy and also tears of sadness, and expansion and contraction. It is the Yin and Yang of life. What's important is what you do with it.

Your inner being has been waiting for you to listen truthfully to the pureness within. You are powerful beyond your comprehension, and have more than strength. You have the power of pure energy within you to be, to do, to have, to accomplish, and to become your dream. When I realized how powerful I was created to be, I stopped feeling small. I rid myself of unnecessary fears, choosing instead to be one with the moment. I learned to breathe moments out of love, peace and joy, and to share it with you and everyone around me. Let me help you heal. Allow me to guide you into that place of discovering and once and for all Honor Your Inner Treasures. Your life will be transformed.

www.honoryourinnertreasures.com

www.limitlessbeliefs.com

www.celinatioauthor.com

Awakening Your Healer Within

The Miracle of You

PHILIP YOUNG

In this book you will glean information from "authorities" who offer mind-expanding ideas and concepts that will benefit your entire life and wellbeing. After countless hours of extensive study, thousands of client sessions, and twenty-five years experience, I am excited to be an authority. In my case, the particular subject of expertise is energetic healing and, like the other authorities in this book, I am pleased to share some of this information and knowledge with you. When learned and understood correctly, energetic healing has the ability to uplift, enlighten, and heal either you or a loved one.

To begin, we must define energetic healing. This is a metaphysical healing that takes place beyond the limits and assumptions of physical science known today. In reading this, you will learn how your inner, non-physical energy affects your health and wellbeing, and how this non-physical energy can be harnessed to assist you, sometimes in miraculous ways.

Today, most people see good health as something that is outside of their control, something that they have to fight to maintain. Health is also usually seen as that which is administered to them by outside medical experts and specialists, but there is another approach. What would it be like if, instead of seeking immediate traditional medical assistance, we embraced and recognized the body's own infinite wisdom? Could we then make changes from within? As people are able to open their minds to it, the answer to this question is most emphatically yes. All the wise and experienced physicians I've met with agree that, even with the scientific knowledge that has been gained over the years, we still know very, very little about the complexities of the human body. We are just beginning to scratch the surface of the miracle that we are.

The point of mentioning how little we know is to emphasize that there is another way of being, a way that truly 'does no harm' and is ultimately within your own control and power. If chosen, this is a path that leads to a radiant, healthier, and happier life that will help fill you with greater joy and wonder than ever before experienced.

Let's start with history. In ancient times it was understood that the natural state of human beings was one of vibrant health, and that this vibrant health came from the Self within. As science progressed, facts and data began to take precedence and this inherent knowledge was lost, buried, changed, or distorted. Now, millennia later, these truths are slowly being rediscovered.

I'd like to suggest that the secret of your entire health lies within you, and it is something that you can control with intention. It is something to be conscious of and to take responsibility for. This is a concept seldom taught or understood, which is especially regrettable because it takes so little commitment and discipline. In much the same way as other daily habits become routine, such as brushing your teeth, taking control of your health can be just that easy.

Many people regard themselves as victims or survivors of a disease (dis-ease), and this attitude has been encouraged in various ways in our society. It is a viewpoint that diminishes the Self and gives power to others. As you begin to consider yourself empowered as an active director of your own health, you engage your mind, spirit and body with intent, allowing miraculous changes to occur.

Every moment of every day, millions of cells are being created perfectly within your lungs, your organs, and your blood. All this takes place at the will of non-physical energy and is without any conscious effort on your part. It occurs simply by your inherent desire and intent. This is a monumental clue to the Truth and the beginning of realizing that you already are a miracle! This non-physical energy fills and actually enlivens your cells, tissues, and even your DNA. In fact, it permeates your entire being. Without being too esoteric, think of it as a 'Life Force', one that ultimately gives you Life and also determines your level of health and wellbeing. In circumstances when your health may not be currently optimal, this energy may have been compromised in some way. However, with help, application and some minimal training, it can be redirected to once again be a positive and beneficial resource for your body.

The dilemma that we have in our limited and often blinkered western way of looking at the world is that this non-physical energy has yet to be measured by material instruments. Society as a whole believes that, if something can't be measured, it cannot be. This line of reasoning actually mimics that of well-meaning priests from medieval times, who might have rigorously dismissed the concept of radio waves simply because they did not have the means to measure them at the time. That way of thinking is archaic. Non-physical energies can be perceived by those who are trained and considered to be attuned, open, and intuitively gifted. Moreover, the effects of these energies can be seen and experienced by all, whether or not we are aware of them.

For many years I have had the good fortune to help people experience healings that have been described as miraculous and even impossible. The people who have experienced healing have been able to reach a certain place within them of greater possibility. The process felt so natural, gentle, and effortless for them that they were often not even consciously aware of it taking place. In much the same way that you can use a magnifying glass to ignite kindling or paper, with my assistance people are able to reach a place of perfect health, a place Within that they ordinarily could not reach on their own.

So, how on earth do you reach the place Within that is already perfect? It is similar to tuning in to a radio station. In this case, however, you are tuning in to a subtle part of your Self. Continuing the radio metaphor, you may well experience some static, but if you persist you are able to tune in to that perfect part of you. As you invite the energy to come forth, hold a strong and consistent intent. Don't give up. When people struggle with this, occasionally they'll recall how they were when they were little children: carefree, happy, and hopefully in perfect health. A child's mind is filled with the exact joyfulness, openness and trust you are seeking. By holding onto these memories, the process may be easier.

To tune in to this station, it is also important to maintain a conscious feeling of gratitude for your perfect health in this very moment, regardless of present outward appearances. It's also important to suspend the activities of the intellect and ego and to control the mind chatter. You must move gently and in a state of deep relaxation through your feeling Self and through your loving Heart. By allowing yourself to maintain this thankfulness and gratitude for the miracle that you are, you can continue to fine tune this channel of perfection.

Because the process is unfamiliar, it can seem difficult at first. Most people find it far easier to begin with my help, and they always have beneficial results when they do. This occurs simply by my being fully Present with individuals in each visit with them. I speak with and listen to each person with patience and compassion. Using the vibration of my voice, and the heat and healing touch of my hands both on and around my clients' bodies, I'm able to help them find that place of perfection that's Within.

Over the years, I have found that there are always emotional hurts and concerns (real or imagined) that affect the wellbeing of the individual. Often, there are few if any people who have the time, patience, or compassion, and who are willing to listen to these concerns, much less respond in a supportive and loving way. Many doctors and specialists I meet sadly agree that they only have a few minutes to spend with each patient. Seldom do they learn much about the individual's hopes, past, fears, loves, concerns, personalities, relationships or families. So for them, if that were the case, it just wouldn't be possible to determine how non-physical energies may be of help to those in need.

When I meet clients in need of non-physical healing I allow the vibration of unconditional Love and highest intention to come forth. These energies can be felt as heat in my hands. Sometimes people actually think I have electric heating pads placed on their body. My own body becomes very warm, even hot, as these non-physical energies flow. It is a process of surrendering, of trusting without any ego whatsoever. Something much, much greater is present and in control. Usually this occurs for about an hour and then the energies stop, as the individual is complete. It is much the same way as we stop pouring water into a glass when it is full. No more can be added for the time being.

I feel most blessed to share these deep, sacred insights into the world of each individual. It allows for another aspect of their health, wellbeing and hope to blossom forth and then they feel better. True healing has to consider the totality of the person. It's a matter of body, mind, and spirit.

The following pages chronicle a few of the positive results I've obtained during my many years of practice. These anecdotal accounts demonstrate how real people have experienced wonderful results during healing sessions. Remember, if one man, woman, or child can do it, then so can another! Perhaps you are seeking a remedy at a time when other choices seem dim. If so, it could be that I might be able to help you or a loved one in some way. Whatever the reason, our Hearts and minds have crossed here for a sacred reason. I do hope that you enjoy the material on these pages and that you are inspired to implement the ideas for yourself, or perhaps to share them with others. Within the sanctity and authority of your own Self, take Heart, remain hopeful, and have faith that another way is surely at hand.

BREAST CANCER

"Your breasts are all clear."

Many years ago a dear and beloved friend called one day to say she had breast cancer. Little did I know then that her journey would help me embark on my own journey to becoming a healer.

Trish had been diagnosed with breast cancer and she was dreading the usual medical approach of "cut, poison, and burn" that still today seems to be the one size fits all medical standard. She had been endeavoring to learn as much as possible about her disease, including various alternative ways to treat her condition. She was fearful of chemotherapy's associated toxicity and the side effects that she knew would be so debilitating for her long-term health and wellness. She was open to another approach that was not harmful to her.

After many years of my own esoteric studies and interests, I was now faced with the stark reality of speaking my truth and endeavoring to do something for her or saying nothing while still trying to be supportive. Many of us have often found ourselves in similar situations. It's a matter of walking the talk vs. talking the talk.

I asked Trish if she was willing to try some healing after she had a lumpectomy. She answered yes and was, in fact, willing to try anything that might help. One day we sat down on her cottage lakefront and, to the bemusement of her husband and my wife, began to try a healing process I had read about. I felt certain and hopeful that I could really help her. That day, for about an hour we held the first of several such sessions, not really knowing what to expect, but highly desirous of a good outcome. Although these were just early steps at the time, nonetheless the good outcome arrived! Her breast cancer disappeared completely and to this day, over 20 years later, her breasts are cancer free!

LIFE SENTENCE

"We can't understand it. The tumors are gone."

Several months later I received a phone call from Jillian, a woman referred to me by Trish. Jillian had cancer throughout her body and had been diagnosed as only having a month or two to live. She was told to go home and get her affairs in order. We arranged to meet at her home and we spoke at length about what was going on in her life.

For the first five weeks we gently dealt with some personal issues that she had experienced. On each visit as I spoke with her I laid my hands upon her as she went into a deep guided relaxation. She returned to the hospital for follow up scans and tests, much to the amazement (and even anger, she said) of her medical doctors, as she had defied their diagnosis. Her tumors were either shrinking or had disappeared completely! Over the next several months she and I continued her healing sessions to the point where all tumors were completely gone.

I continued to see Jillian occasionally for over a two-year period. Years later, she eventually passed, but her life and vitality had been extended so much to the everlasting joy of her family, friends and loved ones.

COMA

"Your daughter is going to be in a permanent vegetative state. We are sorry, but there is no hope."

I happened to meet Rita by chance in an office where she was working. Rita told me her daughter Katrina had been struck by a car and had been thrown 70 feet. She had severe head trauma and had been in a coma for several weeks and, at this point, it was expected by the doctors that she would be in a permanent vegetative condition. There was nothing more they could do for her.

When I was a little boy I experienced head trauma and have always felt a deep sense of compassion and empathy for those who have head injuries. When Rita told me about Katrina, I knew that I had to see her. Out of the blue, I asked Rita if she would be open to that and she said yes.

The next day, walking down the corridors of the hospital, part of me was asking what in the world I was doing there. Part of me wanted to get out of there before I made a complete fool of myself. And yet, another part of me was serene, sure, and calm. I felt like something was guiding me.

Rita was already in Katrina's room and we exchanged a few words. The doctors would not know what I'd be doing, but a couple of the nurses had been informed so that we would not be disturbed quite so much. Seeing Katrina so unresponsive on her bed was quite unsettling. What was I going to say to her? How could this possibly work without a verbal exchange? Without any feedback? With no clues from the eyes? Then I felt a still, calm knowing within me that became my guide. I moved the bed out from the wall, leaned over, and put my hands gently on first Katrina's head, then arm, then hand. Her mom simply looked on, accepting. After about 45 minutes, the healing session seemed to be complete. I really didn't know what to expect. This was new territory for me.

A day later, Rita phoned me to tell me that Katrina had moved her thumb and that the doctors had said this was a reflex. I replied that this is exactly the type of reflex we wanted! A few days later I went back to the hospital and repeated the session, gently touching her arm, her heart, as well as her head. Rita phoned again with good news; this time that Katrina had moved her arm. When I checked my messages a couple of days later I heard one from Rita. Katrina had spoken! I was so overjoyed to hear that and tears ran down my face. It was Christmas Day – what a gift! I saw Katrina several more times and I'm so thrilled that she made a full and quite miraculous recovery.

BRAIN BLOOD VESSEL PROBLEMS (AVM)

"I could drop dead at any moment."

Len was recommended by a friend after he was told by the medical specialists that he had a very serious malformation in the thalamus of his brain. The condition is called an arterio-venous malformation or AVM. There was a weakening in the walls of the blood vessels feeding this very intricate and important region of the brain and he was enduring terrible headaches and some numbness in his extremities. His doctors explained that the medical treatment for such a condition was gamma knife brain surgery. If he survived at all, he could have many cognitive deficits. If he did nothing, he left himself at risk of the malformation erupting and of inevitable sudden death. The odds were against him.

I was his last resort and our first meeting was brief. He was short on time and clearly short on inclination to believe in non-physical healing. He told me that he also had tendonitis from playing golf and wondered if I could do something for that, too. Before long he was soon on the massage table in a deep sleep-like state.

I thought things had gone well and after an hour brought him back. He said he felt unusually relaxed, yet he also seemed to be skeptical as to what he had just experienced. Not surprising for such a practical left brain thinking, alpha male. Still, he was very gracious and we said our farewells.

Sometimes, clients will call me soon after our sessions to let me know their good news. I hadn't heard from Len for several weeks and I was beginning to think that perhaps things had not gone so well for him, but then my phone rang. "Hi Philip, it's Len. I've been meaning to call you. The numbness in my extremities that I'd had for two years was gone the very next day after our session. Also, my stress was relieved and my tendonitis is completely gone too! Most importantly, I had another follow up MRI and the malformation has apparently shrunken from the size of a quarter to the size of a dime. The need for surgery has been averted."

The doctors apparently were astonished by the outcome. They said it was impossible.

Over the following year or two, I heard from Len asking for my assistance on a few other matters, including on behalf of a friend who had hurt her right shoulder ten years previously and could find no relief. She called me the very next day after that session. "I don't know what you did, but all the pain is now gone."

EPILEPSY

"I could black out at any time. I'll never drive or ride again."

Christine and I first met in a metaphysical/spiritual bookstore. We had lots in common and we became great friends. She is also into fitness and health, with a thriving home-based business on a ranch north of Toronto. In addition to caring for her animals, one of her greatest passions is driving a Harley Davidson. Recently, she had been experiencing epileptic seizures and was on strong medications to try and keep the unpredictable seizures under control. The prospect of no longer being able to drive or ride was a huge issue for her.

She was open to having some healing sessions, so I went to her ranch. Christine had three sessions, all of which went well. She now has a full and normal life, teaches yoga, and continues to ride her beloved Harley!

BLOCKED SALIVA GLAND

"I can't eat or drink. The pain is unbearable."

It was a bleak Monday evening in early December. The door opened slowly to reveal a tall, elegant young woman. I smiled and introduced myself and her eyes searched my face for a fleeting second, looking for…what? Hope, perhaps? With a wince of pain, she smiled back slightly.

We sat in her living room and, after exchanging pleasantries, she described her medical condition. Judy could not eat and could barely drink. On a pain and discomfort scale she was at a 10 plus. Her sub-mandible saliva gland duct was blocked with a large stone nearly 6mm (¼ inch) in size. The gland had also become infected. A prominent ENT (ear, nose, and throat) specialist had tried unsuccessfully in a two-hour operation to surgically remove the stone. She sought second opinions and all the ENTs had told her that the only medical recourse was to have her entire saliva gland removed. As a doctor herself she knew that a life without a saliva gland would also be intolerable, not to mention that there could also be permanent nerve damage to her face. She simply had to explore another avenue of possibility, no matter how outlandish it might seem, and thus the call to me.

Judy and I continued to speak at length about what was and had been going on in her life, recently and in the more distant past. A discomfort in her neck and jaw had been part of her life for nine years that seemed to worsen during emotional upset and stress. To me there was an obvious connection, but often the person suffering does not see it.

Judy seemed to be open to the possibility of non-physical healing, so after about 45 minutes we began. With some soothing music playing, I spoke quietly to her as she lay on my healing table. Slowly, she drifted away into a sleep-like state while I placed my hands gently on, around, and above her jaw, mouth, and neck. We ended our session and agreed to meet again in two days. I provided her with some positive thoughts and affirmations to focus on before our next session, that would allow the conscious and unconscious mind to do their parts to support the process further.

When we met again Judy's spirits seemed brighter and she was excited to report that the pain she had been experiencing had reduced significantly from a 10 to a more tolerable 4. She was no longer taking any Percocet for the pain.. During our talk, Judy said that her concerns were now more with the blockage and swelling under her tongue and the discharge from the infection. She rated both of these as a 9 out of 10 on the misery scale.

I reminded Judy of the miraculous being she was already and emphasized that in each and every moment her physical body was performing millions and millions of complex functions without any conscious effort on her part. Her Essential Self was taking care of all these functions. I suggested that this is a part of her that is not generally known to the conscious mind, the ego, or intellect. On the table once again, she drifted off into a relaxed sleep-like state while the energies flowed gently and lovingly in and around her being. As we completed, we again agreed to meet in two days time.

On my third visit Judy told me that after our last meeting she had run to the bathroom and had to spit something out. Amazingly, she was also able to eat again! Judy was excited to tell me that the misery index for the swelling under her tongue and the infection was now only at a 2! The pain had gone. There was only a small bubble under her tongue and only a very slight discomfort on the left side of her neck.

I spoke to Judy a few weeks after that session. In the intervening time, she had had new x-rays that came back with the following reading: No calculi. The stone was completely gone!

ACID REFLUX

"For a long time I experienced the constant threat and misery of acid reflux disease."

Roy, a vital and distinguished gentleman, came to me at age 89. He had suffered with acid reflux for a long time, including a dreadful burning in his throat and stomach, and an appalling taste in his mouth. He had to be very careful about what and when he ate and would often be awakened during the night with great pain and discomfort. Roy's medical doctor had prescribed endless amounts of Gaviston pills for the symptoms but offered no actual remedy. The pills did little to relieve the unrelenting pain, discomfort, and burning sensation. The acidic, acrid taste in his mouth continued to be intolerable.

I asked Roy if he would like to have a healing session right there and then, where he stood chatting outside. He readily agreed (although he was concerned about what the neighbors might say!) I stood next to him and put my hand on his solar plexus and on his back. Right away, the energies began and I started to feel the familiar heat. We stood there for about 10 minutes and then we were complete.

The next day Roy reported that he had slept right through the entire night and that the burning feeling and taste was totally gone. In just one 10-minute session the condition completely disappeared!

It has been over a year now and Roy continues to be free of all the former acid reflux pain and discomfort and can pretty well eat whatever he likes.

"I'm overjoyed now to report that after just a few minutes with Philip, my discomfort has all but vanished!! It has truly been a life-changing experience for me. Philip is a miracle worker!"

SHOULDER AND NECK PAIN

"I don't know what you did, but my pain has been completely cured."

Whitney attended a special restorative yoga class of about a dozen people, where I was able to spend about six or seven minutes with each participant in a healing class setting. She reported that, in just those few minutes, I was able to completely heal her long-standing shoulder and neck problems.

KNEE PROBLEMS

"I can hardly walk, I can't skate. All my practice will be wasted."

Mary was a pre-teen figure skater. She had been unable to skate for some time due to a nasty fall. Her parents took her to physical therapists and specialists throughout the Toronto area with no success. Now, her father brought her to me, literally carrying her in. I spoke with Mary as she lay on a couch while her dad sat outside by the window enjoying the afternoon sun. As I spoke to her and put my hands on her knees and legs, she drifted off into a deep relaxation. After about an hour she was complete and said she felt as if she had been on a wonderful vacation and gave a vivid account of all kinds of beautiful colors while in this dream-like state. The next day, her parents were dumbfounded as they watched her perform skating jumps with ease.

Mary said, "After I saw you, I could walk again, and the very next day I was actually doing figure skating jumps for the first time in five months. I am not going to miss the nationals after all. Thank you so much!"

TEETH AND ROOT CANAL

"I have terrible tooth pain. Another root canal will cost me thousands!"

Over the years, Clare had had a number of painful and expensive root canals. Recently, the pain began again and her dentist recommended yet another. Clare had received a number of healing sessions from me for other health and wellness concerns and, when I asked her, said she was open to trying some healing on her jaw and teeth as well.

As she lay back deeply relaxed on her couch, I gently cradled her right jaw and touched her lower molars. After about an hour, we were complete and the next day, the pain had gone. Clare cancelled the root canal procedure with her dentist and is problem-free to this day. In just one session we eliminated the pain and we eliminated the issue.

FOOT PROBLEMS

"I'm afraid my life is over."

Hanna had severe foot problems and was not able to walk properly. Her job of 25 years required her to be mobile and on her feet all day so this issue was completely debilitating. When we met, I spoke to Hanna and explained to her about the strength and power of non-physical energies. I touched her arm and heart. After that the pain in Hanna's feet went away.

Hanna says, "I thought my life was over because I could not walk. If I couldn't walk I would not be able to work. Now I can walk pain-free again. You are my savior! I am so grateful. Thank you!"

CHEST PAIN AND FIBROID TUMORS

"All my life I have been in pain. Now, I feel wonderful."

Kaitlin is a nurse. She had experienced severe and unrelenting pain in her upper chest all her life. There was no known medical cause found, even after every type of medical test had been conducted. She also had dreadful pain in her lower abdomen due to two inoperable fibroid tumors. After her first healing session, the pain in her upper chest left completely. After the second, the intolerable pain in her lower abdomen disappeared.

Kaitlin says, "Now I feel wonderful! Thank you!"

There are, of course, many, many more anecdotes covering almost every imaginable type of malady, but this is all the room we have for now. As the authority on energy healing, I hope that you have found this chapter to be helpful as an introduction to such an expansive metaphysical topic. The concepts may be new to you, although the principles have always been used, in every part of the world, throughout history.

If you feel that I may be able to assist you or a loved one, please call me in Toronto at 416-447-9550. If there is a good fit with us and we do work together, I will visit you in the privacy of your own home and I will commit to working with you until you are completely well again. In the meantime, may blessings of Love and Light always be upon you.

Thank you for your interest! You can learn more at www.PhilipYoungHealer.com

www.ingramcontent.com/pod-product-compliance
Lightning Source LLC
Chambersburg PA
CBHW060603210326
41519CB00014B/3559